MARIANNE MOORE

Marianne Moore

AN INTRODUCTION

TO THE POETRY

GEORGE W. NITCHIE

COLUMBIA UNIVERSITY PRESS

NEW YORK & LONDON

for Lucy and Wylie Sypher

*George W. Nitchie is Professor of English at
Simmons College in Boston, Massachusetts.
ISBN 0-231-03119-x Clothbound
ISBN 0-231-08312-2 Paperbound*

*Library of Congress Catalog Card Number: 79–96998
Printed in the United States of America*

Foreword

There is no easy introduction to an introduction to the poetry of Marianne Moore, for she is unique. No one else sounds like her. And because her rhetoric is so distinctively her own, no one is likely to want to sound like her. It is easy, for example, to show the "influence" on modern poetry of men as different as William Carlos Williams, Ezra Pound, W. B. Yeats, and T. S. Eliot. Devices they have used have been adapted by other men to other ends. But to be "influenced" by Marianne Moore's devices would be to produce conspicuously imitative work. Her extreme peculiarities isolate her from her admirers, preserve her from founding a tradition.

Mistress of quirks and oddities, Marianne Moore writes poems that look like nothing so much as a magpie's nest of precisely fitted trivia and that almost inevitably surprise us by or into abrupt, oblique, and superficially capricious generalizations. Her home truths, her moral assertions seem to relate in something other than a cause-and-effect way to the material she has assembled. Neither pertinent nor altogether impertinent, those outrageous accuracies seem, when she is in top form, really to have animated a world of pure fact until that world, like one of the gods laboring a thought, gives birth to figures that are heroic, intractable, pure. In her characteristic work, the commonplace assumes a regal strut.

Inimitable, she is also unpredictable. Her revisions—such as the spectacular reduction of "Poetry" from an initial thirty lines to a final three—exasperate some readers and delight others. But they also serve to remind us that, for the living poet who sees his work as indigenously part of himself, the poem is likely to continue to change whenever the poet changes. When he no longer wants to tinker with it, it may be dead. There is no doubt at all in Miss Moore's mind that the best thing to do with a poem that is not living is to discard it. As she notes in the one-sentence Author's Note to the *Complete Poems,* "Omissions are not accidents."

And yet that discarding of past work, for someone as frugal of words and objects as she is, must cost Miss Moore a good deal of psychic energy. Averaged out over her sixty-some productive years, the 120 poems of *Complete Poems* represent a fraction less than two poems a year. It is no wonder that so conservative a writer chooses to go on polishing those poems that interest her.

Accepting her for what she is—a lady of quirks and craft and genius—Mr. Nitchie traces her evolution from witty, shy upstart to deeply committed, sensitive observer of a world that seems tottering always on the rim of self-destruction. In the face of what may be universal disaster, she offers us primary values, a poetry of plain fact transmuted—at its best —into wisdom. Admiring the unique, the odd, the peculiar, she reminds us that these qualities—conspicuously her own— make life worthwhile. It is these qualities that make Brooklyn's "crowning curio," the Camperdown elm, worth preserving, and that may preserve, if we are lucky enough and curious enough and possessive enough, the world's other crowning curio, us.

Preface

This study of Marianne Moore's poems has no formal thesis
to urge; it is, as its subtitle indicates, an introduction to the
poetry. But it ends with tribute paid to Miss Moore by a
distinguished younger contemporary, a tribute that is at once
personal and public. Praising her in verse for her integrity and
in prose for an art that bespeaks personal goodness, W. H.
Auden sees her as exemplary, if not to a nation then at least
to other poets and to their readers. And this book shares
Auden's bias. Despite an unevenness in her poetry—and what
poet's work is not uneven?—despite what seem to me to have
been errors in judgment about particular poems, and periods
of time in which her impulse to write was somehow divided
against itself or misdirected, Miss Moore provides us with a
work that takes its responsibility seriously, yet regards itself
with neither vanity nor portentousness. One need not apolo-
gize for partisanship.

The book owes a good deal to writers other than Miss
Moore, as the Notes and the List of Works Consulted indicate.
I am particularly aware of three books to which I am indebted
in a degree that may not show sufficiently: A. Kingsley Weath-

erhead's *The Edge of the Image,* which gave focus and articulation to ideas that would otherwise have remained shapeless; Bernard F. Engel's *Marianne Moore,* which by coming first provided a text to argue or agree with; and Eugene P. Sheehy and Kenneth A. Lohf's *The Achievement of Marianne Moore,* which I have consulted again and again for bibliographical information. For matters of biography and personal insight, articles and published interviews by Donald Hall, George Plimpton, and Winthrop Sargeant have been indispensable. And to Professor John Unterecker of Columbia University, who suggested that I write the book in the first place, and Mr. Robert Watts, reference librarian of Simmons College, who tracked down the early texts of many poems Miss Moore subsequently revised or abandoned, I am personally grateful.

Unless otherwise accounted for in the text or notes, all of Miss Moore's poems from which I have quoted or to which I have made reference will be found in *The Complete Poems of Marianne Moore,* published jointly in 1967 by The Macmillan Company and The Viking Press. It is perhaps unnecessary to add that there would be singularly little profit in reading what Robert Graves calls the snivelling commentary without the thundering text.

GEORGE W. NITCHIE

July, 1969

Contents

CHAPTER 1

Some Question of Integrity

Marianne Moore has been quoted as saying that her biography, if it is ever written, will be "a very tame affair," [1] and there seems little reason to doubt her judgment. A trip to Paris with her mother in 1911, and two or three other trips abroad during the years since then; involvement with avant-garde writers, if perhaps as something of an outsider ("Alfred Kreymborg was not inhibited. I was a little different from the others. He thought I might pass as a novelty, I guess." [2]); five years in the late 1920s as staff member and editor of *The Dial*, "the most distinguished literary monthly in the U.S. to champion modern artistic movements";[3] prizes, awards, honorary degrees; consultation by the Ford Motor Company for advice, not taken, in naming its ill-fated Edsel (among her suggestions, Pastelogram and Utopian Turtletop[4]); respect, friendship, affection from a circle wide and various enough to include T. S. Eliot and James T. Farrell, Allen Ginsberg and W. H. Auden, Robert Frost and Ezra Pound, John Hersey and Robert Lowell, Amiya Chakravarty and M. J. Tambimuttu; translation into German, French, Spanish, and Italian; publication not only in little magazines and literary quarterlies but in *The New Yorker, Harper's Bazaar, Seventeen, Vogue, Life,* in publications of Abbott Laboratories and the Steuben Glass Company, and on page one of the *New York Herald Tribune,* where "Hometown Piece for Messrs. Alston and Reese," concerning the then Brooklyn Dodgers, appeared on opening day of the 1956 World Series;[5] distinction, work, a fastidious and orderly delight in life and literature, and an attractive though never flagrant eccentricity, but nowhere much drama or visible excitement. For thirty-six years she lived in the same apartment on Cumberland Street in Brooklyn and attended the same Presbyterian Church on Lafayette Avenue; in 1954 she changed publishers, however, and in the winter of 1965–1966 moved from Brooklyn to Manhattan—on the whole, a tame affair, summed up perhaps in W. H. Auden's affectionate and allusive statement, "Marianne, you are one of the very few poets who have never made a fuss, never written *error* with more or less than three r's." [6]

Lack of fuss characterizes a great deal of Marianne Moore's life. Though Hart Crane once characterized *The Dial* under her editorship as a "hysterical virgin" [7] and Ezra Pound quotes her as having written to him, of English politics in the middle 1930s, "I dislike Eden and Baldwin as much as if I knew them personally," [8] she has been neither a forcer of issues nor a focus of literary or personal vendettas. Writing of herself in 1958, she tells us: "Of poetry, I once said, 'I, too, dislike it'; and say it again of anything mannered, dictatorial, disparaging, or calculated to reduce to the ranks what offends one. I have been accused of substituting appreciation for criticism, and justly, since there is nothing I dislike more than the exposé or any kind of revenge." [9] Her published articles and reviews bear out this self-characterization; scrupulously fair, by no means lacking in enthusiasms and preferences, she distinguishes between those she loves (Pound, William Carlos Williams, Wallace Stevens, Pavlova, Henry James) and those she merely accepts (it is not easy to find examples; Jack Kerouac, perhaps, who is "not for prudish persons" [10]) in terms less of what she says of them than of how much; she simply does not write about books and people she does not approve of. "The passion for setting people right," she tells us in "Snakes, Mongooses, Snake Charmers, and the Like," "is itself an afflictive disease," and either that disease has not struck her or she has resisted its ravages extraordinarily well. The principle is that of not making a fuss. Subject to bouts of what her friends call "Marianne's psychosomatic flu," she says, "It's dire! And all that penicillin and other things in bottles! It's like the forcible feeding of an important reptile." [11]

The reptile in question was born in 1887 near St. Louis, Missouri, in the town of Kirkwood, the younger of two children. Her engineer father, John Milton Moore, faded from the picture before her birth, victim of a business failure and a consequent nervous breakdown from which he made no satisfactory recovery; she never saw him. [12] Her mother, Mary Warner Moore, daughter of the pastor of the First Presbyterian Church in Kirkwood, undertook the upbringing and education of both children; the son, John, became himself a Presbyterian clergyman and naval chaplain, and Marianne graduated from Bryn Mawr in 1909 and from the Carlisle (Pennsylvania) Commercial College in 1910. She had hoped to major in English and French, but Bryn Mawr found her insufficiently apt in these subjects, and she reports spending most of her time in the biology laboratories, at one point thinking of studying

medicine. Carlisle led directly into teaching commercial subjects in the United States Indian School there, where for three
and a half years she was in charge of the commercial depart-
ment and, apparently, of tennis. In one capacity or the other,
she had as a student Jim Thorpe, the Indian athlete, of whom
she recalls: "Once . . . we were walking along railroad tracks
in the heat. I had a gloria man's umbrella. 'Could I carry your
parasol for you?' he said. 'Thank you, James,' I said, 'by all
means.' He was courteous, you see, and very gentle. I liked
him. . . . Of course he had his troubles." [13] Years later she was
to praise a Brooklyn clergyman for being "imaginatively inconclusive." [14]

Some of her poems were printed in the Bryn Mawr undergraduate literary magazine, others in the alumnae magazine,
but except for reading, which she preferred to teaching commercial subjects, she had no special contact with the world
of contemporary letters until 1915, when *The Egoist,* in London, and *Poetry: A Magazine of Verse,* in Chicago, both printed
poems of hers. The event may have been prophetic; at any
rate, both periodicals were much involved in the effort to
publish, and if necessary to create, a body of authentically new
writing, both had connections with Ezra Pound, and both were
to acquire legendary status among little magazines. *Poetry,* for
example, gave T. S. Eliot (also born in St. Louis, less than a
year after Marianne Moore) his first publication by printing
"The Love Song of J. Alfred Prufrock," and in the same year
of 1915; *The Egoist* published James Joyce when no one else
would and was under Eliot's managing editorship during its
last two distinguished years of existence. At least as far as "new
poetry" periodicals go, Miss Moore began at the top.

Then in 1916, when her brother accepted a pastorate in Chatham, New Jersey, she and her mother moved to Chatham; a year or two later, the pastor having become a Navy chaplain, they moved to New York City, where they shared an apartment on the Lower East Side until the 1929 move to Brooklyn. As was true of the move to Chatham, family circumstances were involved this time also; John Moore had been assigned to the Brooklyn Navy Yard, and living together as a family evidently mattered a great deal to all three Moores. In 1952 Wallace Stevens wrote to Norman Holmes Pearson that Marianne Moore "belongs to an older and much more personal world: the world of closer, human intimacies which existed when you and I were young—from which she and her brother have been extruded like lost sheep. As a matter of nature they stick together." [15] A similar degree of closeness clearly prevailed between mother and daughter, who speaks of consulting freely with Mrs. Moore about her poems and of following her advice. *Selected Poems,* when it was issued as a separate volume, included a postscript: "Dedications imply giving, and we do not care to make a gift of what is insufficient; but in my immediate family there is one 'who thinks in a particular way'; and I should like to add that where there is an effect of thought or pith in these pages, the thinking and often the actual phrases are hers." [16] *Collected Poems* is dedicated "To Mary Warner Moore 1862–1947." [17]

The move to New York was also a move into what might be called active literature, when she first met and mixed with writers. Asked whether moving to New York led to more writing than she otherwise would have done, she replied: "I'm sure it did—seeing what others wrote, liking this or that. With me it's always some fortuity that traps me. I certainly never intended to write poetry. That never came into my head. And now, too, I think each time I write that it may be the last time; then I'm charmed by something and seem to have to say something. Everything I have written is the result of reading or of interest in people, I'm sure of that. I had no ambition to be a writer." [18] New York, as she put it in her poem of that name, offered "accessibility to experience," and that included making the acquaintance of such people as Alfred Kreymborg, William Rose Benet, Elinor Wylie, William Carlos Williams, Hilda Doolittle (whom she had known vaguely as a classmate at Bryn Mawr without realizing she was interested in writing), Lola Ridge, Marsden Hartley, and a good many others, including the publishers of *The Dial*, Scofield Thayer and Sibley Watson. (Sibley Watson and his wife, Hildegarde, share the Dedication in *A Marianne Moore Reader*, and the poem "The Wood-Weasel" is an upside-down acrostic on "Hildegarde Watson.") Whether she intended to write poetry or not, she was writing it, and it was being published and even sought after. At a party held by Lola Ridge, who "had a large apartment on a ground floor somewhere," Miss Moore was induced to read a poem she had written. "And Scofield Thayer said of my piece, 'Would you send that to us at *The Dial*?' 'I did send it,' I said. And he said, 'Well, send it again.' That is how it began, I think." [19] Her association with *The Dial* went rapidly from contributor, to award winner, to acting editor, then to editor, a position she held from 1926 until 1929, when Thayer and Watson decided to stop publishing.

During this time she taught in a private school for a while and, from 1921 to 1925, worked as an assistant in the Hudson

Park Branch of the New York Public Library, both of which positions, she thinks, "hardened my muscles considerably, my mental approach to things." [20] And meanwhile two friends, Hilda Doolittle and Winifred Ellerman ("Bryher"), more convinced than she that her poems merited permanent form ("Desultory occasional magazine publication seemed to me sufficient, conspicuous enough." [21]), had prepared a selection of twenty-four poems that was published in 1921 by the Egoist Press in London under the title *Poems*. The volume was produced without Miss Moore's knowledge, but she was grateful for the gesture ("The chivalry of the undertaking." [22]), which put her in that distinguished company of American poets— Robert Frost, Ezra Pound, T. S. Eliot—whose first books did not find American publishers.

Her second book [23] changed all that. *Observations*, which contained most of the contents of *Poems* and a number of additional poems, appeared in 1924, prepared for publication by Miss Moore and published by the Dial Press. The following year *Observations* received the Dial Award of two thousand dollars (at that time Eliot was its only other recipient, for *The Waste Land*) and its author joined the staff of *The Dial*. The work clearly delighted her; she recalls "a visiting editor's incredulity when I said, 'To me it's a revel,' after being asked if I did not find reading manuscript tiring." [24] Equally clearly, it left her little time for her own writing; she has indicated that, for her, tasks interfere with one another,[25] and she suspects that the decision to discontinue publication of *The Dial* was reached by its publishers out of "chivalry . . . because I didn't have time for work of my own." [26] She is much readier to ascribe chivalry to others than talent to herself.

Selected Poems (1935) indicates both that she had found time for work of her own and that she was a genuinely international phenomenon; the volume was issued by Macmillan in New York and by Faber and Faber in London, both editions including a laudatory introduction by T. S. Eliot. Two years previously she had received from *Poetry: A Magazine of Verse* its Helen Haire Levinson Prize of one hundred dollars; in 1935 she received the Ernest Hartsock Memorial Prize; in 1936 she published *The Pangolin* in England and, in 1941, *What Are Years?* in New York. In 1941 came the Shelley Memorial Award of one thousand dollars, and in 1944 she published *Nevertheless*. By the middle 1940s she was clearly an eminence; in 1944 she received the Harriet Monroe Poetry Award of five hundred dollars and the Contemporary Poetry Patrons' Prize; in 1945, a Guggenheim Fellowship; in 1946, one of six annual grants of one thousand dollars from the National Institute of Arts and Letters, becoming in 1947 one of the Institute's 250 members and in 1955 a member of the American Academy of Arts and Letters, the Institute's inner circle of 50 members. In 1948 the *Quarterly Review of Literature* devoted an entire issue to critical discussion of Miss Moore and her work. In 1949 she contributed to *T. S. Eliot, A Symposium*, prepared in Eliot's honor by Richard March and M. J. Tambimuttu, and in that same year she received an honorary Litt. D. from Wilson College, the first of many such academic recognitions. The following year, 1950, brought a second Litt. D., from Mount Holyoke, and an L.H.D. from Smith. In 1949 her poem "A Face" was published separately in a limited edition, and by 1950 there were five recordings of Miss Moore reading her poems, with two more appearing in the 1950s.

In 1951, at the age of sixty-four, she published her *Collected Poems,* drawing together, often with substantial revision, most of her earlier published poems and adding a group of nine "hitherto uncollected" items. As volumes of collected poems go, it was small, running to less than 150 pages of text, but size was belied by distinction; for this book Miss Moore received the Pulitzer Prize, the National Book Award for poetry, and the Bollingen Prize, the three carrying a total money value of twenty-five hundred dollars. In 1953 came the Gold Medal Award of the American Academy of Arts and Letters, "for distinguished achievement in arts and letters as shown in the entire work of the recipient." [27] The procession of honorary doctorates continued—from the University of Rochester in 1951, from Dickinson College in 1952, from Long Island University in 1953—and in 1953 Bryn Mawr honored her with its M. Carey Thomas award and a visiting lectureship.

Miss Moore in her sixties and seventies has been astonishing. In 1945 she collaborated with Elizabeth Mayer in translating Adalbert Stifter's *Rock Crystal, A Christmas Tale.* Perhaps coincidentally, in that same year, as she recalls it, "W. H. Auden was asked by a publisher what classic he considered had been neglected. . . . He thought La Fontaine's 'Fables' and suggested me as the one to do the translation. I thought he was the one to do it, but he claimed he hadn't the patience." [28] She apparently did, for nine years. "I worked practically all the time. . . . I'd wake up at six o'clock and get right to work, and I'd keep at it all day and all evening, except for an occasional brief stop to eat, or maybe I'd have to go to the market and buy a few odds and ends. Then back to the job again. I did the whole thing over completely four times." [29]

While she was working on the "Fables," the publisher who had commissioned the translation died; the Macmillan Company, publishers of *Selected Poems, What Are Years?, Nevertheless,* and *Collected Poems,* decided against the project and advised her to " 'put it away for a while.' 'How long?' I said. 'About ten years. . . .' " [30] She found such Horatian advice depressing, but in 1953 and 1954 separate fables found publication in *Yale French Studies, Encounter, Poetry, Harper's Bazaar, Partisan Review, Kenyon Review, Accent, Hudson Review, Harper's Magazine,* and *Chicago Review,* among others; in 1954 the Viking Press issued the entire collection, in both limited and trade editions; and in 1955 Faber and Faber in London issued a *Selected Fables.* Reviewing the fables, Hugh Kenner declared: "Miss Moore's solid achievement is . . . to have discovered the principles of a badly needed idiom, urbane without slickness and brisk without imprecision. Since Chaucer's fell into disuse, English verse, constantly allured by the sonorous and catechristic, hasn't had a reliable *natural* idiom that can imitate the speech of civilized men and still handle deftly subjects more complex than the ones whose emotions pertain, like Wordsworth's, to hypnotic obviousness; hence nothing existed for a La Fontaine to be translated into." [31] And in 1955 Caedmon issued a recording of Miss Moore reading eight of the fables and thirteen other poems.

Meanwhile she was being translated as well as translating. As early as 1928, Eugène Jolas had included a French translation of "A Grave" in his *Anthologie de la nouvelle poésie américaine,* and in the twenty years following, a handful of other poems ("England," "The Fish," "In Distrust of Merits," "The Monkeys," "Poetry," "Silence," "A Talisman," "To a

Snail," "To a Steam Roller," and "What Are Years?") were translated into French, Spanish (in both Spain and Latin America), and Italian, appearing in periodicals and anthologies. In 1954 Limes Verlag in Wiesbaden published a bilingual edition of thirty-one poems from *Selected Poems* and *Collected Poems*, with a translation of Eliot's preface, under the title *Gedichte: Eine Auswahl.* This German recognition had its French and Italian counterparts in 1964, when both a Paris edition of *Poèmes* and a Milan *Omaggio a Marianne Moore* appeared.

In 1955 she published *Predilections,* a collection of reviews, lectures, and other prose pieces; became a member of the American Academy of Arts and Letters; engaged in extended correspondence with the Ford Motor Company as it attempted to find an appropriately magical name for its new car; and received a Litt. D., her sixth, from Douglass College of Rutgers University. In 1956 she issued *Like a Bulwark,* a small collection of eleven previously uncollected poems, all but one ("Bulwarked against Fate") postdating *Collected Poems*; made a second recording for Caedmon; and took part in inaugurating the Ewing Lectures at the University of California. In 1958 she received her second L.H.D., from Pratt Institute. In 1959 she published *O to Be a Dragon,* a collection of fifteen poems for the most part previously uncollected, though "To a Chameleon" had appeared in both *Poems* and *Observations,* and "I May, I Might, I Must" went back to her undergraduate days under the title "Progress." In 1960 she received the Gold Medal of the Poetry Society of America. In 1961 she was chosen as the feature performer in Chicago's Poetry Day, an event initiated in 1955 "to aid the Modern Poetry Association and the magazine *Poetry*. . . . On Poetry Day the poet thus honored reads his verse to a large audience in the afternoon and in the evening is a guest of honor at a dinner and literary auction";[32] her predecessors here were Robert Frost, Carl Sandburg, John Crowe Ransom, Archibald MacLeish, T. S. Eliot, and W. H. Auden. In 1962 she published *The Absentee,* a dramatic version of Maria Edgeworth's novel, and *Eight Poems,* 195 signed copies of which were issued by the Museum of Modern Art with hand-colored drawings by Robert Andrew Parker; and in 1962 the National Institute of Arts and Letters observed her seventy-fifth birthday with a dinner meeting in her honor.

The year 1963 was marked by another limited edition, *Occasionem Cognosce: A Poem,* 175 signed copies of which were issued by the Stinehour Press in Lunenburg, Vermont; another venture in translation, this time three tales of Charles Perrault; the text for a catalog of an exhibit of paintings by William Kienbusch; and an award for outstanding achievement in poetry from Brandeis University, in the form of a medal and fifteen hundred dollars. In 1964 came the French and Italian translations of her poems mentioned above and *The Arctic Ox,* published in London by Faber and Faber once more. In that same year forty-six friends and admirers contributed to a *Festschrift for Marianne Moore's Seventy Seventh Birthday,* edited by M. J. Tambimuttu, and again in that same year Bernard F. Engel, of Michigan State University, published his *Marianne Moore,* the first book-length consideration of the poet and her work. In 1965 she told Donald Hall, "People study my face and say, 'Do *you* still *write?*' Of course I do. Why not?"[33]

Two years later she remarked to Jane Howard, of a recent photograph:

"I'm all bone . . . just solid, pure bone. I'm good-natured, but hideous as an old hop toad. I look like a scarecrow. I'm just like a lizard, like Lazarus awakening. I look permanently alarmed, like a frog. I *aspire* to be neat, I try to do my hair with a lot of thought to avoid those explosive sunbursts, but when one hairpin goes in, another seems to come out. Look at those hands: they look as if I'd died of an adder bite. A crocodile couldn't look worse. My physiognomy isn't classic at all, it's like a banana-nosed monkey." She stops for a second in thought. "Well, I do seem at least to be awake, don't I?" [34]

Obviously she was. In the two years before this remarkable piece of self-evaluation, she had put together *A Marianne Moore Reader,* issued her most limited limited edition (*Silence,* of which twenty-five copies were printed by L. H. Scott in Cambridge, Massachusetts), and received a five-thousand-dollar fellowship from the Academy of American Poets, all in 1965, and in 1966 she published *Tell Me, Tell Me,* a collection of poems and prose pieces. In August, 1967, she was still sufficiently awake to receive the MacDowell Medal of the MacDowell Colony for Creative Artists in Peterborough, New Hampshire, the first woman to receive that award.[35] Bemedaled, beprized, and bedoctored, she was eighty years old. And in November, 1967, timing the event to coincide with her birthday, Macmillan and Viking jointly issued the inaccurately titled *The Complete Poems of Marianne Moore.*

Honors and distinctions do not seem to have made a great deal of difference, however, except perhaps for bringing more people within her orbit than would otherwise have been the

case. Shortly after her move to Manhattan in 1966, she told a
writer for *The New Yorker,* "I receive fifty letters a day, and
answer almost all of them." [36] On the same occasion she also
said, "I think that the more you respect people the more you let
them alone. I'm a metropolitan recluse." And perhaps she
would really like to be, if she were permitted, or could permit
herself. But she apparently cannot. To a *Life* reporter, she has
admitted to two-hour telephone calls and an inability to keep
from talking,[37] and Winthrop Sargeant, George Plimpton,
Bernard Engel, and others have testified to her remarkable
capacity for sustained conversation. Engel observes that "in
one three- or four-minute passage she can move from praise of
a scholar in English from Belgrade to commendation of a
dramatic version of E. M. Forster's *A Passage to India,* then to
her enjoyment of a lecture by Thornton Wilder, and to favor-
able remarks about Theodore Roethke's teaching in Seattle; on
to praise of Karl Barth; and finally to mention of criticism of
her writing at Bryn Mawr. . . . All this she knits together, in
this instance the theme being the need for clearness in expression." [38] Sargeant separates her listeners into two groups,
"those who delightedly occupy themselves in smelting out a
memorable simile or adjective, and those who complain that
it requires an enormous amount of strenuous concentration to
make any sense at all of what she is saying." [39] Plimpton finds
her talk "engrossing," but "almost as anarchic as that of Casey
Stengel," [40] and notes the fine surprise of her remark in Yankee
Stadium on a major league baseball player, "standing back
from the plate and leaning easily on his bat as the action developed at second base. 'He is simulating *sang-froid.*'" [41] "I'm
inclined to worry about people," she says. "I keep thinking

have they enough money? are they happy?" [42] Perhaps it was this aspect of Miss Moore that Wallace Stevens made reference to when he wrote of her in 1952, "The more I see of her the more certain I am that some question of integrity enters into everything she does and is decisive of it for her." [43]

Has she enough money? Is she happy? The questions are not only banal and impertinent but probably hopeless as well. Gracious with her interviewers, amiable and responsive and even voluble, she is not fascinated by herself and she does not give herself away. "I don't study out what I say, I just talk," [44] she says, and though this description seems consistent enough with her published interviews and television appearances, nevertheless it may mislead. Winthrop Sargeant notes that "she is as scrupulous in her regard for good form as the heroine of a Jane Austen novel," [45] and Jane Austen heroines do not prattle or expose themselves unduly; Sargeant adds, in fact, "there is about her a suggestion of both the Puritan woman and the Prussian knight." Like one of her own armored animals, she has her means for self-protection, both in her life and in her art; I shall pay attention to some of them in the following chapters.

CHAPTER 2

The Courage of Our Peculiarities

"Feeling at its deepest—as we all have reason to know—tends to be inarticulate. If it does manage to be articulate, it is likely to seem overcondensed, so that the author is resisted as being enigmatic or disobliging or arrogant. . . . we must be as clear as our natural reticence allows us to be." [1] So wrote Marianne Moore in 1944, and again: "Voltaire objected to those who said in enigmas what others had said naturally, and we agree; yet we must have the courage of our peculiarities." [2] She knew whereof she wrote, for in large part she was writing about herself, about her own practices and preferences, her own sense of obligation to her poems, to their language, and to the limited but real public they had acquired during the thirty-odd years since they had first begun to appear in print.

That sense of tension between the responsibility to be clear and an apparently inescapable degree of obscurity, between the natural and the enigmatic, has dogged Marianne Moore for a long time. In a 1966 article commissioned by the *Christian Science Monitor,* she tells us: "Always, in whatever I wrote—prose or verse—I have had a burning desire to be explicit; beset always, however carefully I had written, by the charge of obscurity. Having entered Bryn Mawr [in 1905] with in-

tensive zeal to write, I examined, for comment, the margin of
a paper with which I had taken a great deal of trouble and
found, 'I presume you had an idea if one could find out what it
is.' " [3] She also recalls a similar experience at a reading of her
poems ("verse," to use her own self-deprecating term; "what I
write . . . could only be called poetry because there is no
other category in which to put it" [4]) before a women's club
in New Jersey. As she reminds us in one version of "Poetry,"

> we
> do not admire what
> we cannot understand,[5]

and she does not blame us for our refusal.

It would be absurd to deny that Marianne Moore is fre-
quently obscure, enigmatic, or peculiar; it would be still more
absurd, however, to suggest either that such characteristics
seriously interfere with an enjoyment of her poems, even
those in which the courage of her peculiarities is most in evidence, or that patience and familiarity are any less effectual
with her than they are with Eliot, Emily Dickinson, or Donne.
And to place Miss Moore among such poets is, in kind if not
always in degree, to place her among her peers—among poets
of formidable intelligence, formidable wit, and formidable
eccentricity, poets who characteristically achieve their effects
through surprise and the strategic violation of decorum. We
may observe both characteristic degrees of peculiarity and
characteristic devices of intelligently eccentric wit in the behavior of three of Miss Moore's cats, in "Bird Witted," "Peter,"
and "The Monkeys."

"Bird-Witted" raises its problem clearly; everything turns on a word, which converts observation and anecdote into something different from either. The anecdote is beautifully clear and self-contained. Young mockingbirds, full-grown and handsome to look at but still unable to fly or feed themselves, and endowed with voices like "the high-keyed intermittent squeak/ of broken carriage springs," are threatened by a cat. The mother bird, her own voice grown harsh with the cares of parenthood, comes to the rescue,

> nerved by what chills
> the blood, and by hope rewarded—
> of toil—since nothing fills
> squeaking unfed
> mouths. . . .

She "half kills" the cat—a wry, rueful, and amusing observation about birds and perhaps people—and that is all. Or almost all. Actually, the mother bird

> wages deadly combat,
> and half kills
> with bayonet beak and
> cruel wings, the
> intellectual cautious-
> ly creeping cat.

And "intellectual" jumps out at one, the single word in the poem that takes the reader by absolute surprise, compelling him to a reassessment of what he has read.

What, in fact, has he read? A remarkably concrete observation of a commonplace backyard event? A fable in praise of passionate feeling over intellectual singlemindedness? Something of both, certainly. The first collection of Miss Moore's poems published under her own supervision was entitled *Ob-*

servations, and the tendency to look at things and to be grat-
ifyingly concrete about what she sees has been persistently
characteristic. She is, as Randall Jarrel has noted, *"the* poet
of the particular." But she is also, he adds, "in our time, *the*
poet of general moral statement." [6] Concrete observation leads
to fable or exemplum; for Miss Moore, the two are all but
inseparable. To observe a jerboa is to consider the excellent
and the corrupt in civilizations; to observe a cat stalking
fledgling mockingbirds is to consider relationships to life.
Writing of elephants in "Melancthon," she asks,

> will
> depth be depth, thick skin be thick, to one who can see no
> beautiful element of unreason under it? [7]

In "When I Buy Pictures," she insists that

> Too stern an intellectual emphasis upon this
>   quality or that detracts from one's enjoyment.

And praising William Carlos Williams she writes, "The 'ability
to be drunk with a sudden realization of value in things others
never notice' can metamorphose our detestable reasonableness and offset a whole planetary system of deadness." [8] To
find reasonableness detestable and to see it embodied in a
stalking cat may strike one as gestures of eccentricity, but "a
sudden realization of value in things others never notice," or
at least may not notice without prodding, precisely describes
the effect of seriously witty surprise that Miss Moore produces
by labeling her cat "intellectual."

Value in things unnoticed may be present here in another
form as well, equally eccentric, and in evidence to a greater
or lesser degree depending on whether one has read the poem

by eye or by ear. Read by ear alone, "Bird-Witted" sounds like lucidly observant prose; it has no conspicuous rhyme, and its rhythms are rhetorical rather than metrical, a matter of cadence rather than line or foot. Looked at on the printed page, it consists of six ten-line stanzas, each stanza duplicating the pattern of indentation established in the first. Looked at somewhat harder, the stanzas follow a consistent rhyme scheme; in each stanza, lines one, three, and six rhyme with one another, as do lines two and four, and five and ten—ABABCAXXXC. And looked at harder yet, the stanzas have their own consistent system of prosody that stands revealed not by counting feet as in most regular English verse but by counting syllables— nine for each first line, eight for each second, and so on, giving a pattern 9864736474, with only three anomalous lines, two of them light by one syllable each, and the third heavy by two syllables, so that the poem's total syllable count is precisely what it would have been had each stanza been precisely regular. One may reasonably ask, "Who cares?" and the answer has to be, "Miss Moore."

"Melancthon" may be to the point again with its question, "will depth be depth . . . to one who can see no beautiful element of unreason under it?" The question seems to be rhetorical, both in and out of context. "Beautiful element of unreason" describes equally well the monumental calm of an elephant or a mother mockingbird's frantic courage in defending her fledglings; and it may describe a rigorously followed prosodic system whose rhyming is often inaudible ("solemn" rhymes with "them," "dressed" with "modest," "uneasy" with "the") and whose metric can be experienced for the first time only by stopping to count. "This carefully idiosyncratic counting," writes Hugh Kenner, "corresponds to the poet mind-ing her own business without actually fussing to keep it a secret."[9] It says that, although conspicuous artificiality is to be avoided, rigor, discipline, and precision are important both for mockingbirds and for people who write, or read, poems. Reviewing a book on Goethe, Miss Moore writes: "We see his spiritual independence, his love of liberty as 'the opposite of coercion, but not the opposite of a voluntary subjection to such coercion as that of moral discipline, or that of metrics, or social forms, or reasonable law'—a concept embodied in his saying, *'Und das Gesetz nur kann uns Freiheit geben.'* "[10] The cat in "Bird-Witted" makes no such voluntary subjection of himself to coercion; the mockingbird and Miss Moore do.

"Peter" depends less on abrupt surprise than does "Bird-Witted," but the "sudden realization of value in things others never notice" is as characteristic of the one poem as of the other. Peter, concretely identified in a note as a "cat owned by Miss Magdalen Hueber and Miss Maria Weniger," sleeps, dreams, and entertains himself, in all things behaving like a cat. Miss Moore observes and reflects; precise observation of particular details ("the detached first claw on the foreleg corresponding/ to the thumb, retracted to its tip") passes into general moral statement ("When one is frank, one's very pres-ence is a compliment").

And yet strategies differ in the two poems. In "Bird-Witted" we have no particular sense of the poem as fable until the very end, when "intellectual" drops it on us—all of it and all at once. "Peter" creeps more cautiously; the movement from fastidiously precise observation to moral statement begins no later than line twelve:

> Sleep is the result of his delusion that one must
> do as well as one can for oneself,
> sleep—epitome of what is to him the end of life.

And it may begin in the opening lines:

> Strong and slippery,
> built for the midnight grass-party
> confronted by four cats,

which suggest that Peter may be a product of design in a purposive universe. In either case, the poem moves easily back and forth between its two modes in what Charles Tomlinson has called "a high seriousness that refuses to be merely solemn," [11] and its cat, limited by hedonic delusions, nevertheless demonstrates integrity in being, without pretense, exactly what he is. "We must be as clear as our natural reticence allows us to be," [12] Miss Moore has told us, and Peter is an absolute case in point:

> It is clear that he can see the virtue of naturalness,
> that he does not regard the published fact as a surrender.

More explicit in its moralism than "Bird-Witted," though no less witty, "Peter" exhibits the same praise of an instinctive naturalness that does what it must with a minimum of wasted effort and a minimum of fuss.

"The Monkeys" moralizes also, but more astonishingly and unnervingly than either of the other two poems discussed so far. Observed details of monkeys, zebras, elephants, small cats, and parakeets contribute an impression of magnificence to a remembered visit to a zoo. But the only thing that really happened on the visit, the only thing that is more than a remembered detail of appearance or behavior, was a short address on esthetics delivered by a wholly unforgettable cat, "that Gilgamesh among/ the hairy carnivora":

> "They have imposed on us with their pale
> half-fledged protestations, trembling about
>   in inarticulate frenzy, saying
>   it is not for us to understand art; finding it
>   all so difficult, examining the thing
>
> as if it were inconceivably arcanic, as symmet-
> rically frigid as if it had been carved out of chrysoprase
>   or marble—strict with tension, malignant
>   in its power over us and deeper
>   than the sea when it proffers flattery in exchange for hemp,
>   rye, flax, horses, platinum, timber, and fur."

This is peculiar in at least two ways. First, though talking animals are common enough in the tradition (and Miss Moore has translated La Fontaine), they are not common in Miss Moore, despite her use of animals as exempla: "Melancthon," spoken by an elephant, and this poem are the principal exceptions, and "Melancthon" has vanished from the canon. Second, and more problematic surely, there is little in "The Monkeys" that prepares us for the cat's observations.

> It is difficult to recall the ornament,
>   speech, and precise manner of what one might
>   call the minor acquaintances twenty
>   years back

suggests that "speech," the various animals' various remarks, may be among the forgotten details of the visit to the zoo, but even this does not provide altogether fair warning of what we have coming to us. One's first impression of the cat's speech is that it is devastating, brilliant, and unrelated to anything except some wholly eccentric authorial whim—that it borders in fact on the private joke. Not even familiarity with the poem wholly counters this impression, if personal confessions are permissible. The impression, I believe, is wrong but understandable, and an understanding of its wrongness can be useful in coming to an understanding both of Miss Moore's intelligence and of her eccentricity.

I suspect that part of the impression derives, at least for me, from expecting a kind of consistency from Miss Moore that she does not always offer or intend. The cat in "Bird-Witted" is clearly less admirable than is the mother mockingbird; and in "Peter," though the cat is admirable in his feline way, it is a finite admirableness. But in "The Monkeys" the Gilgamesh-cat, who is also a Dr. Johnson-cat, gives every indication of speaking with authority, and the point of course is that cats have no single role to play in Miss Moore's bestiary, at least with regard to being right or wrong.

This lack of a fixed role would probably matter less in "The Monkeys" if it were clearer just what the cat is in fact saying and how we are to take it, whether the cat is a spokesman for values that Miss Moore herself recommends to us or whether the cat is a cat, speaking out of his own moral and esthetic felinity. The question is less simple than it seems, and that may well be the reason why Miss Moore has allowed it to stand. The position about which the cat is being catty is one that Miss Moore herself has found unsatisfactory; like the cat, she deplorers excessive obscurity ("How obscure may one be? And I suppose one should not be consciously obscure at all." [13]), pretentiousness ("these things are important not because a/ high-sounding interpretation can be put upon them but because they are/ useful." [14]), and critical arrogance ("If he must give an opinion, it is permissible that the/ critic should know what he likes." [15]).

And yet it is less than clear that we are to take all this straight. The speaker is an extraordinarily practical cat in his view of art, a view that sees art as essentially a commodity market, proffering "flattery in exchange for hemp,/ rye, flax, horses, platinum, timber, and fur." [16] Art is not difficult, it is not highly organized, it does not involve strict tensions, and it has no particular power or depth; it is a luxury to exchange for other luxuries. This is not an intrinsically absurd or improper idea of art, and in fact it has a good deal in common with what seems to be Miss Moore's own idea. "So art," she writes, "is but an expression of our needs; is feeling, modified by the writer's moral and technical insights." [17] "Needs" are presumably met by marketable commodities, and the expression of human needs may be regarded as a form of flattery and an indulgence in luxury. Winthrop Sargeant tells us that Miss Moore not only "bears no ill will toward the world of business, finance, and technological progress," but "regards it as an interesting and worth-while world, and gladly concedes that some of its activities are quite possibly even more interesting and worth while than the writing of verse." [18] She has confessed to wishing that she had invented the collapsible dustpan.[19]

All of which is to say that the cat has a case. But one peculiarity of most Marianne Moore poems is that they are symmetrically rigid, if not frigid, that they are "strict with tension" between the prose elegance of the thing said and the verse elegance of formal regularity ("The Monkeys" rhymes aaxbxb and manifests a syllable count in its stanzas of 15,16, 10,10,15,11 with only one anomalous line). Of such tensions, it may be said with absolute literality that "it is not for us to understand art," since whatever it is that makes us respond to such tensions is a matter not of understanding but precisely of response, something probably organic in nature rather than rational—a "beautiful element of unreason." And this suggests that the cat's case is less that of Miss Moore against the critics than of Miss Moore against Miss Moore. That "Gilgamesh among/ the hairy carnivora" is the cutter of Gordian knots, the reducer of nonsense, the practical, common-sense Marianne Moore who, as we all know, has said of poetry, "I, too, dislike it." But she has also said, once more, that art is feeling and that "feeling at its deepest . . . tends to be inarticulate." [20] Or as in the poem "Silence," "The deepest feeling always shows itself in silence;/ not in silence, but restraint." And this is not Gilgamesh, who is neither silent nor restrained in his comments, and whose feelings give no indication of tending to be inarticulate.

Thus "The Monkeys" appears to be less dogma than dialogue, with one voice silent—not silent, but restrained. The cat's speech is not irrelevant, gratuitous, or whimsical; it appears to be so, if it does, only because Miss Moore has adopted the "inconceivably arcanic" device of providing no rebuttal against a brilliantly articulate spokesman for a position that she does not simply endorse, that is as limited in its way as those of the less articulate monkeys, zebras, and elephants.[21] "I shall not forget him" means not that he is right but that he is memorable and that he is a working part of that combination of disparate elements, Marianne Moore, a peculiarity that she must and does have the courage of, though it is not the only one.

Two or three general observations suggest themselves on the strength of this short view of three poems. In the first place, event and anecdote in Marianne Moore's writing are rarely presented either for their own sake or for the sake of their unadorned intensity. Those happenings that she observes or invents, that seem to her the appropriate stuff of poetry, interest her because they embody or suggest values, ideas, or modes of conduct. Rather than let sleeping cats lie, she finds in them occasion for comment on the life of man, and she is willing to risk a considerable degree of obliquity in the process of making them give up their significance; her moralities are seldom as straightforward and uncomplicated as that of the grasshopper and the ant, for instance. On the one hand, she has, as moralist, a taste for aphorism; on the other hand, the aphorisms tend to appear in contexts that limit their applicability:

As for the disposition invariably to affront,
an animal with claws should have an opportunity to use them,

and this is something less than a categorical imperative, even for animals, not all of whom have claws. Such an interest in ethics is exploratory, conditional, and even experimental rather than absolutist or dogmatic; Miss Moore detects ethical implications in conduct, but she does not necessarily advocate all she detects.

In the second place, the interest in ethics is matched by an interest in art. Art, once more, is "feeling, modified by the writer's moral and technical insights," [22] and it may be worth noting that moral insights modify feeling rather than the other way round; that is to say that when Miss Moore is thinking explicitly of her role as artist, moral insight is not primary. Any of the three poems looked at thus far will bear this out. The moral judgment of "Bird-Witted" depends on the event and the empathy developed therewith; "The Monkeys" is explicitly about art rather than ethics; and it is a fair question whether the attitude in "Peter" is moral approval or esthetic appreciation. In a 1944 essay on Anna Pavlova, she writes of Pavlova's "sense of style," which is "also a moral quality," [23] and the equation suggests both Peter and the Gilgamesh-cat of "The Monkeys." As they did for Keats ("Though a quarrel in the Streets is a thing to be hated, the energies displayed in it are fine." [24]), ethics and esthetics have a symbiotic relationship throughout Miss Moore's body of work. There is not much question which of the two is finally prior for her as a person. In a 1950 *Partisan Review* symposium on "Religion and the Intellectuals" she writes of "the moral law (which is self-demonstrating, most of us admit)," [25] and she is always deprecatory about art, at least her own; asked by Donald Hall in 1961, "At what point did poetry become world-shaking for you?" she replied, "Never!" [26] But it has clearly been an absorbing game for her; during her bouts of writing, Winthrop Sargeant reports, "she has likened herself . . . to 'a cat in a basket with the lid on,' 'a badger under a hedge of poison ivy,' and 'a rat in a cheese,'" [27] all of them evidently enjoying themselves tremendously, if self-indulgently, in the process of modifying feeling by their moral and technical insights.

And in the third place, prosody. Marianne Moore has written poems in traditional metrical forms ("To Military

Progress," for example) and others in what may as well be called free verse ("New York"). But more frequent and more characteristic are those written in the peculiar prosody of "Bird-Witted" and "The Monkeys," with stanzas based on syllable count and inconspicuous rhyme working against a cadence that is essentially that of elegant and precise prose. Quite simply, there is no one among her contemporaries who writes in quite this way. The point here is not really that of having a voice and manner of one's own, though Miss Moore surely has one, as characteristic and individual as that of Frost or Auden, for example. But the prosody has little to do with the voice because it is never more than partially heard, and this is not accidental. Miss Moore remarks on "my own fondness for the unaccented rhyme," attributing it to "an instinctive effort to ensure naturalness," and again, "concealed rhyme and the interiorized climax usually please me better than the open rhyme and the insisted-on climax. . . ." [28] Perhaps even more revealing, "I have a passion for rhythm and accent, so blundered into versifying. Considering the stanza the unit, I came to hazard hyphens at the end of the line, but found that readers are distracted from the content by hyphens, so I try not to use them." [29] Her judgment may or may not be sound here; I am not sure which is more likely to distract a reader, the hyphenation in "The Fish," emphasizing rhyme in lines one and two of each stanza:

> All
> external
>   marks of abuse are present on this
>   defiant edifice—
>   all the physical features of

>   ac-
>   cident—lack
>   of cornice. . . .

or the discovery of concealed rhyme in "A Carriage from
Sweden":

> No one may see this put-away
>   museum-piece, this country cart
>   that inner happiness made art;
> and yet, in this city of freckled
> integrity it is a vein
>
> of resined straightness from north-wind
>   hardened Sweden's once-opposed-to
>   compromise archipelago
> of rocks. Washington and Gustavus
> Adolphus, forgive our decay,

in which syllables three and eight in each first line of a
stanza rhyme (may-aw*ay*, res*ined*-wind) as do the first and
last syllables in each last line (*in*tegrity-vein, Adolphus-dec*ay*).
Either way, such rhyming is eccentric, but there is no question
of its not having been intended; it testifies not to a defective
ear but to a prickly and rigorous, perhaps almost an obsessive,
concern for craft.

Such a concern for craft is risky but not unprecedented;
there is in fact a plausible case to be made that sees Marianne
Moore as occupying one of the two possible attitudes, at least
for poets in English, toward a relatively strict prosody. Roughly
speaking, one may cooperate with one's prosody or one may
set oneself in opposition to it. Shakespeare's Sonnet 73 ade-
quately illustrates the first attitude.

> That time of yeeare thou maist in me behold,
> When yellow leaves, or none, or few doe hange

Upon those boughes which shake against the could,
Bare rn'wd quiers, where late the sweet birds sang.
In me thou seest the twi-light of such day,
As after Sun-set fadeth in the West,
Which by and by blacke night doth take away,
Deaths second selfe that seals up all in rest.
In me thou seest the glowing of such fire,
That on the ashes of his youth doth lye,
As the death bed, whereon it must expire,
Consum'd with that which it was nurrisht by.
This thou percev'st, which makes thy love more strong.
To love that well, which thou must leave ere long.

Each line here approximates recognizably the theoretically normal iambic pentameter line. The approximation is, to be sure, more or less. As with all "regular" verse, one probably hears two things in a reasonably sophisticated reading of this sonnet: the actual movement of the line as speech, and beneath it the counterpointed movement of the ideal iambic rhythm, never quite corresponding to what the ear hears but never or seldom stretching the relationship to the breaking point; "hearing" a meter is a matter of constant adjustment and readjustment of what is there in fact to what would be there in theory.

Beyond the matter of lines, the poem cooperates even more closely with its prosody. Prosodically, the sonnet breaks naturally into three equal quatrains and a concluding couplet; rhetorically, it breaks into three metaphorical assertions and a moralizing conclusion. Prosodic components and rhetorical components correspond; form and content harmonize in a straightforward and, within the limits of this discussion, relatively uncomplicated way.

Milton's sonnet "On the late Massacher in Piemont" works differently.

> Avenge O Lord thy slaughter'd Saints, whose bones
>   Lie scatter'd on the Alpine mountains cold,
>   Ev'n them who kept thy truth so pure of old
>   When all our Fathers worship't Stocks and Stones,
> Forget not: in thy book record their groanes
>   Who were thy Sheep and in their antient Fold
>   Slayn by the bloody *Piemontese* that roll'd
>   Mother with Infant down the Rocks. Their moans
> The Vales redoubl'd to the Hills, and they
>   To Heav'n. Their martyr'd blood and ashes so
>   O're all th' *Italian* fields where still doth sway
> The triple Tyrant: that from these may grow
>   A hunder'd-fold, who having learnt thy way
>   Early may fly the *Babylonian* wo.

Individual lines here probably approximate the iambic norm about as closely as do Shakespeare's; but Milton's sonnet, more sparing in its prosodic resources (Shakespeare allows himself seven rhyme sounds, Milton only four), is more conspicuously and artificially a prosodic entity in its husbanding of those resources. Yet the speech movement of the whole poem seems to deliberately ignore its prosodic organization. Ten of Milton's lines have no terminal punctuation, as against only one of Shakespeare's; rhetorical pauses and metrical pauses, that is, do not coincide. And while Shakespeare's rhetorical units correspond exactly with the prosodic form of three quatrains and a couplet, Milton's first quatrain, or its rhetorical equivalent, runs over into the fifth line; his second stops in the middle of line eight, doing visible violence to the strong prosodic break between lines eight and nine, where the rhyme sounds change; and the sonnet concludes with two unequal sentences, neither of which corresponds with any prosodic element except at the conclusion of the last line, where such correspondence is unavoidable. That harmony of form and content evident in the Shakespeare sonnet is in Milton, if not a dissonance, at least a radically strained counterpointing. Shakespeare cooperates with his prosody, Milton opposes it.

In this admittedly limited sense, Marianne Moore is more Miltonic than Shakespearean—more Miltonic in fact than Milton. Milton does not bury his systematic rhymes as does Miss Moore in some instances, and while he counts syllables quite as scrupulously as she, he also maintains at least diplomatic relations with an iambic pentameter norm. She does not, nor with any other norm that the ear can detect; her stance of opposition to her prosody is as complete as she can make it. As R. P. Blackmur remarks, "The fact of syllabic pattern has a kind of tacit interest, but we cannot say whether we can appreciate it, because we do not know whether even the trained ear can catch the weight of variations of this order." [30] It is only by deliberate counting of syllables, by a mode of reading so artificial as to be grotesque, that one recognizes ten syllables in one line and thirteen in another, repeated through a series of stanzas. And this calls for more attention than it has so far received.

Marianne Moore's attitude toward her own prosody—more accurately, perhaps, since she never seems to write or talk of prosody per se, toward the prosodic elements of her own work—is peculiar. On the one hand, "Bird-Witted," as we have seen, is characterized by an extraordinary degree of regularity in the syllable count of its stanzas, even making up for two light lines by one extra heavy one. On the other hand, Miss Moore has said: "I never 'plan' a stanza. Words cluster like chromosomes, determining the procedure. I may influence an arrangement or thin it, then try to have successive stanzas identical with the first. Spontaneous initial originality—say, impetus—seems difficult to reproduce consciously later." [31] On the one hand she tells us, "I like the end-stopped line";[32] on the other hand, "Bird-Witted," though six of its nine sentences do end at the end of a line, characteristically breaks its lines between an adjective and its noun, a preposition and its object, an adverb and its verb, and on four occasions between the elements of a compound word ("meek-/coated," "flute-/sounds," "sun-/lit") or between a root and its suffix ("cautious-/ly"). We note the strictest sort of formal regularity and a statement indicating an essentially casual attitude toward such regularity, an expressed preference that sounds almost Popean and a practice that flies in the face of such a preference. It is not easy to detect in all this a single attitude.

Nor, perhaps, is it necessary. Probably no prosody, regular or otherwise, performs a single function, evokes or expresses a single attitude. For Miss Moore, it seems clear that her prosody expresses a fastidious dislike of sprawl, either verbal or emotional; a sense that cadence alone is not a sufficient safeguard against such excesses; a compelling taste for schematic arrangements of things, indicated not only in counted syllables but in orderly patterns of indentation in her left margins; an equally compelling taste for the freer arrangements and patterns of highly skilled talk (like Samuel Johnson and Oscar Wilde, she is herself an extraordinary and eccentric talker); and I suspect most important of all, her moral and esthetic imperative toward discipline, particularly self-discipline, in all things. To Marianne Moore, once more, Pavlova's sense of style was also a moral quality; the essay on Pavlova is a praise of discipline, of values that can be achieved through rigorous devotion of oneself to a craft, and that emphasis provides a constant theme of her critical writing. Of gusto as a literary quality, she writes that it "thrives on freedom, and freedom in art, as in life, is the result of a discipline imposed by ourselves";[33] of T. S. Eliot, "one who attains equilibrium in spite of opposition to himself from within, is stronger than if there had been no opposition to overcome; and in art, freedom evolving from a liberated restraint is more significant than if it had not by nature been cramped";[34] of Sir George Sitwell, "throughout, an inescapable lesson is afforded us—that discipline results in freedom";[35] of Louise Bogan, that she achieves "a transcending of the self through difficulty";[36] and I have already noted her approval of Goethe's *"Und das Gesetz nur kann uns Freiheit geben"* [37]— only law can give us freedom. And for a poet, at least for Miss Moore's kind of poet, law means prosody, those regulations and organizations of language that make possible both the exercise of a more or less impersonal craft and the maneuverings of personal insight and ability through which craft may become art.

To some degree Miss Moore's practice of revising provides confirmation of this view of her attitude toward her prosody. "Poetry" is the most striking case in point of the demands and counterdemands its author has imposed on herself. The astonishing authoritative version, as it appears in *Complete Poems,* consists of just three lines:

> I, too, dislike it.
>   Reading it, however, with a perfect contempt
>   for it, one discovers in
>   it, after all, a place for the genuine.

Even Miss Moore, who rarely annotates her revisions, was apparently uneasy this time, since she includes in the notes what she bafflingly refers to as its "original version," [38] the version that appears in the 1935 *Selected Poems* and in subsequent reprintings and anthologies. That version consists of five stanzas, all constructed of six lines apiece except for the third, which has only five. Rhyme tends to appear in lines two and three (two stanzas out of five) and four and five (four stanzas out of five). All five stanzas have nineteen-syllable first lines and thirteen-syllable last lines, and all but the anomalous third show the pattern 5,8,13 in their last three lines. Second lines vary from thirteen to twenty-two, third lines from seven to nineteen. All stanzas show the same pattern of indentation; all lines one reach to the left margin, lines two and three are slightly indented, four and five indented slightly more, and six slightly more yet. Even the anomalous third stanza minimizes its difference by simply omitting either line four or line five, otherwise preserving the pattern of indentation. But the anomaly persists; the third stanza, at least, wants accounting for.

Observations does not help much. "Poetry" appears there as well, but in a version that has little but phrases in common with later versions:

> I too, dislike it:
> there are things that are important beyond all this fiddle.
> The bat, upside down; the elephant pushing,
> the tireless wolf under a tree,

the base-ball fan, the statistician—
"business documents and schoolbooks"—
these phenomena are pleasing,
but when they have been fashioned
into that which is unknowable,
we are not entertained.
It may be said of all of us
that we do not admire what we cannot understand;
enigmas are not poetry.[39]

R. P. Blackmur has remarked of the difference between this version and that included in *Selected Poems*: "There is the difference between the poem and no poem at all, since the later version delivers—where the earlier only announces—the letter of imagination. . . . The imaginary garden was there but there were no real toads in it." [40] It seems unlikely that anyone would quarrel with that judgment; the *Observations* version looks very much like notes toward a poem, the poem of *Selected Poems*, in fact, which has received that "transcending of the self through difficulty" [41] that Miss Moore has attributed to Louise Bogan. But the particular anomalies remain.

Actually, there is a still earlier version of "Poetry" in the 1921 *Poems*, and this version makes clear a good deal. The text, which has apparently not been reprinted, is as follows:

I too, dislike it: there are things that are important beyond all this
fiddle.
Reading it, however, with a perfect contempt for it, one discovers
that there is in
it after all, a place for the genuine.
Hands that can grasp, eyes
that can dilate, hair that can rise
if it must, these things are important not because a

high sounding interpretation can be put upon them but because
they are
useful; when they become so derivative as to become unintelli-
gible, the
same thing may be said for all of us—that we
do not admire what
we cannot understand. The bat,
holding on upside down or in quest of something to

eat, elephants pushing, a wild horse taking a roll, a tireless wolf
under
a tree, the immovable critic twinkling his skin like a horse that
feels a flea, the base-
ball fan, the statistician—case after case
could be cited did
one wish it; nor is it valid
to discriminate against "business documents and

school-books"; all these phenomena are important. One must make
a distinction
however: when dragged into prominence by half poets, the result
is not poetry,
nor till the autocrats among us can be
"literalists of
the imagination"—above
insolence and triviality and can present

for inspection, imaginary gardens with real toads in them, shall we
have
it. In the meantime, if you demand on one hand, in defiance of
their opinion—
the raw material of poetry in
all its rawness and
that which is, on the other hand,
genuine, then you are interested in poetry.[42]

And this, of course, is what we have been looking for. It manifests virtually no prosodic anomalies. In all stanzas, lines two and three rhyme, as do four and five; all five stanzas have six lines apiece, and the syllable count is a regular 19,22,11,5, 8,13, with only two dubious cases, in the second and sixth lines of the final stanza. For line two to have the canonical twenty-two syllables, one must either pronounce "opinion" with four syllables or suspect that "on one hand" should read "on the one hand," to parallel "on the other hand" in line twenty-nine —as in fact it does in the 1935 version, though there the line is exceptionally irregular, running to only thirteen syllables. Line six has its thirteen syllables as long as "interested" is a three-syllable word; but in the 1935 version "interested" has to have four syllables if the line is to be regular, and the stanzas' first and last lines in this later version appear to be the only abso-lutely fixed points in the stanzaic pattern. Practically speaking, the prosody of the *Poems* version is, as the Gilgamesh-cat of "The Monkeys" put it,

> as symmet-
> rically frigid as if it had been carved out of chrysoprase
> or marble.

Or, as he put it in the *Poems* version of "The Monkeys," entitled "My Apish Cousins":

> as
> symmetrically frigid as something carved out of chrysopras
> or marble." [43]

The same relationship holds between the two versions of this poem as between those of "Poetry"; anomalies in the later version turn out to be regularities in the earlier. The as/chryso-pras rhyme just quoted restores to stanza four a regularity that the preceding stanzas call for and that revision had removed. Other anomalies—an extra line in stanza two and a short fifth line in stanza three—have precisely the same history.

What happened seems clear enough. In *Poems*, prosody was inviolable, though inconspicuous. But the demands of prosody may have betrayed Miss Moore into padding her statement; she evidently thought so, at any rate, and the result was the extraordinarily condensed version of *Observations*, in which there is no suspicion of padding, of prosody for the sake of prosody, because there is no prosody. The demands of law have given way to the demands of naturalness and, oddly enough, of a preference for end-stopped lines. But this version in turn would not do; it neither says what it has to say nor organizes what it has to organize, and *Selected Poems* ac-knowledges the error. Here one recognizes, with hindsight wisdom, that almost every change from the *Poems* version re-moves dead or neutral verbiage or makes inaccuracy accurate. Of the first sort is the conspicuous excision in stanza three of "case after case/ should be cited did/ one wish it," which is true but empty, or in stanza five of "in defiance of their opin-ion," when no opinion has in fact been cited. Of the other sort is the change in stanza three from "twinkling" to "twitching" as the term for what the immovable critic does with his skin, a change from the merely cute to the precise, and perhaps that from "autocrats" to "poets," in stanza four. Less clearly func-tional is the relocation, in stanza two, of "the" from the end of line two in *Poems* to the beginning of line three in *Selected Poems*. A terminal "the" is perhaps eccentric, and the change does make possible an end-stopped line, but it also loses the rhyme, and in any case the eccentricity is no more substantial than the unaltered hyphenation in stanza three that produces "the base-/ ball fan" and preserves a rhyme that, in the altered stanza, is no longer needed. The change seems merely whimsical.

But it is the only change that seems whimsical. It is no exaggeration to say that the others can be wholly accounted for in terms of a clear, even a prose concern for sense and economy of language. And if that concern cuts across the other concern for rigidly regular prosodic forms, Miss Moore has evidently preferred, through trial and error, to maintain the double discipline, though flawed, rather than to sacrifice either to the necessities of the other. The flaws are real enough; given Miss Moore's particular prosody, they call attention to themselves more emphatically than analogous irregularities in a more conventional metric; detached from its history, the third stanza of "Poetry" (the *Selected Poems* version) is in its formal aspect irritatingly peculiar. But its peculiarity resembles that which later led her to sacrifice all but three lines of this remarkable poem, then to assign it to a footnote, with subfootnotes of its own. Both peculiarities are of the sort that, Miss Moore insists, we must have the courage of; they testify in their ways to the integrity of her designs.

CHAPTER 3

Additions and Subtractions

Marianne Moore's 1921 book, *Poems,* has never been reprinted, nor did it have an American edition. It is a small book of twenty-four poems on twenty-four pages, handsomely printed at the Pelican Press, 2 Carmelite Street, E.C., London, for The Egoist Press. And to those readers of Marianne Moore who are chiefly familiar with her work through *Collected Poems, A Marianne Moore Reader,* and now *Complete Poems,* it is almost bound to look odd. Eleven of the twenty-four poems do not appear in the 1951 *Collected Poems,* and a twelfth had disappeared from *Complete Poems,* though one of the eleven does reappear in *O to Be a Dragon* and the two later collections with a wildly revised title: in *Poems,* "You are like the realistic product of an idealistic search for gold at the foot of the rainbow"; in the later volumes, "To a Chameleon." Two other poems have had their titles changed considerably; in *Poems* "The Monkeys" was "My Apish Cousins" and "Melancthon" (not reprinted in *Complete Poems*) was "Black Earth." Of the thirteen poems that survive in *Complete Poems,* few are identical with their *Poems* versions. Stanzas are altered, lines are omitted, quotation marks are added or changed, phrasing is revised, and in four cases ("Poetry," "Picking and Choosing,"

"England," and "When I Buy Pictures") *Poems* poems in strict syllabic stanzas are not only revised with respect to phrasing but wholly recast in a kind of free verse.

"Pedantic Literalist," the first poem in *Poems,* is fairly characteristic of those that have survived with minor revision. The most immediately apparent difference between the two versions is their appearance on the page. In *Poems,* indentation proceeds evenly from the first line in a stanza to its last:

> Prince Rupert's drop, paper muslin ghost,
>   white torch—"with pow'r to say unkind
>   things with kindness, and the most
>   irritating things in the midst of love and
>   tears," you invite destruction.

In *Complete Poems,* the pattern is less simple:

> Prince Rupert's drop, paper muslin ghost,
>   white torch—"with power to say unkind
> things with kindness, and the most
>   irritating things in the midst of love and
>   tears," you invite destruction.

Perhaps the later version looks more balanced, less inclined to run off the page, but the difference seems chiefly idiosyncratic. The noticeably artificial "pow'r," of the first version, is dictated apparently by prosodic necessities, as is "roy'l" in line four of the second stanza; the *Poems* version requires eight syllables in all second lines, eleven in all fourth, and in *Complete Poems* these lines are anomalous by virtue of an extra syllable. In *Collected Poems* this move from artifice to naturalness was at least to a degree offset by the trick of beginning all stanzas with a capital, while both *Poems* and *Complete Poems* versions conform to normal prose usage in this respect, with capitals only for the first and second stanzas, where sentences begin. In both *Collected Poems* and *Complete Poems* stanza three alters the structure of a sentence and apparently the substance of a quotation, though either a printer or a proofreader has been at fault in *Collected Poems,* where "painful" comes out "pinful" and one quotation mark has been omitted. And while the last line of the *Poems* version reads "immutable reduction," all later versions give "immutable production," either deliberately repeating the last line of stanza two or else testifying again to inaccurate printing.

Considerably more elaborate is the revision bestowed on "When I Buy Pictures." The *Poems* version consists of five five-line syllabic stanzas with a syllable count of 12,11,15,21, 18, and with second and fourth lines rhyming. The opening stanza is verbally all but identical with the opening lines in *Complete Poems*:

or what is closer to the truth, when I look at
    that of which I may regard myself as the
        imaginary possessor, I fix upon that which would
    give me pleasure in my average moments: the satire upon curi-
                                                          osity,
        in which no more is discernible than the intensity of the
                                                          mood,

the only change being a "what" substituted for an original "that which" in the third line. Further along, however, the *Complete Poems* version omits almost entirely a passage that would, if preserved, have followed line ten:

or that which is better without words, which means
    just as much or just as little as it is understood to

mean by the observer—the grave of Adam prefigured by himself; a
bed of beans
or artichokes in six varieties of blue. . . .

And the last three lines in *Complete Poems*:

It comes to this: of whatever sort it is,
it must be "lit with piercing glances into the life of things";
it must acknowledge the spiritual forces which have made it,

were originally a substantially different stanza:

It comes to this: of whatever sort it is, it
must make known the fact that it has been displayed
to acknowledge the spiritual forces which have made it;
and it must admit that it is the work of X, if X produced it; of
Y, if made
by Y. It must be a voluntary gift with the name written on
it.

In this poem too the principal movement is from verse artifice
toward prose naturalness, but it is also from one kind of statement to another, from a catalog of whims to a statement about
esthetics. The closing lines in *Poems* seem fussy and pedantic
measured against those of *Complete Poems,* though in at least
one detail the earlier version is clear where the later is cryptic;
when a picture "must admit that it is the work of X, if X
produced it," then there is some point in thinking of it as a
more or less "literal biography perhaps—in letters stand-/ing
well apart upon a parchment-like expanse." X has vanished
from *Complete Poems,* but his literal biography remains, to
puzzle painstaking readers.

The ultimate form of revision, however, is abandonment,
and, as we have already seen, almost half of the twenty-four

titles in *Poems* have been abandoned, to the considerable com-
plication of the Moore canon. Thus *Poems* contains twenty-
four poems; *Observations* reprints, often with substantial revision, twenty-one of those, and adds thirty-two others; *Selected
Poems* retains thirty-nine poems from *Observations* and adds
nine more. *What Are Years?* (1941) includes fifteen poems,
none reprinted from earlier collections, though five of them
had appeared in a limited edition, *The Pangolin and Other
Verse,* in 1936; and one, "The Student," had been part two of
"Part of a Novel, Part of a Poem, Part of a Play," the first title
in *Selected Poems,* when that much-parted poem was first
printed in *Poetry: A Magazine of Verse* in June, 1932. Part two
is omitted in *Selected Poems;* in *Collected Poems* the ungainly
collective title disappears, and parts one and three stand on
their own as "The Steeple-Jack" and "The Hero," and "The
Student" is among those omitted from the version of *What Are
Years?* that *Collected Poems* includes, though it reappears in
Complete Poems. Nevertheless (1944) includes six new poems.
And *Collected Poems* (1951), with seventy-one titles, omits
four from *Selected Poems* and four from *What Are Years?,*
adds nine new titles, and as noted above divides one old one.
By 1951, some twenty-five poems had been abandoned along
the way, more than a third of the number retained in *Col-
lected Poems. Like a Bulwark* (1956) adds eleven new titles;
O to Be a Dragon (1959) adds fifteen titles, two of them revised and retitled versions of poems published earlier;[1] and
Tell Me, Tell Me (1966) adds four short prose pieces, seventeen new poems, and "Sun," a considerably revised version of
"Fear and Hope," from *Observations. Complete Poems,* with
one-hundred-twenty titles, restores two abandoned poems,

"The Student" and "To a Prize Bird," which first appeared in *Observations* and was not reprinted in subsequent collections; but the restoration is partially offset by the abandonment of "Melancthon." *Like a Bulwark, O to Be a Dragon,* and *Tell Me, Tell Me* appear intact in *Complete Poems* except for the prose pieces in *Tell Me, Tell Me;* and four later and previously uncollected poems appear as well. Approximately thirty other published poems, most prior to 1921, have never been collected.[2]

"Omissions are not accidents," Miss Moore tells us brusquely in her introductory note to *Complete Poems;* but the reinclusion of such once-omitted poems as "To a Prize Bird," "The Student," "To a Chameleon," and "Sun" suggests that some omissions may have come to seem errors. It is in fact difficult to avoid the suspicion that there has been from the beginning an element of mere compulsive tinkering in her revisions and exclusions, as perhaps there is in any poet. Auden is a case in point, as Joseph Warren Beach has shown;[3] Wallace Stevens' "Sunday Morning" exists in at least two versions;[4] and the variorum edition of Yeats's poems is a monument to inspired and calculated tinkering. But Miss Moore's tinkerings differ from these others'. Stevens' revisions, at least those on "Sunday Morning," were undertaken in consequence of something approximating editorial fiat from Harriet Monroe;[5] Auden's reflect perhaps an awkward attraction toward multiple and imperfectly assimilated roles; and Yeats's accompany and express the deliberate process of converting the poet he had been in the 1880s into the poet he became in the 1920s and 1930s. Miss Moore's express—what?

Often enough one can answer that question satisfactorily of

an individual poem, as we have seen with respect to "Poetry," [6] moving as it does in its successive versions between rigorously symmetrical artifact and quintessential statement, between prose that looks like verse and verse that looks like prose. But in "Poetry" the answer is both exceptional and excessive: one must eliminate elaborate nonsense in order to get to the heart of the matter, but one must save the nonsense one has eliminated in order to provide credentials for what remains. This sounds absurd, but it is difficult to understand the *Complete Poems* strategy with "Poetry" in other terms. And there are other instances that, though less striking, point in the same direction. Thus "When I Buy Pictures," as we have seen, has been transformed from a stanzaic poem to one of quite freely cadenced lines, and in *Complete Poems* the same thing has happened to "Peter," "Picking and Choosing," and "England." But other poems constructed on the same principle of syllabic stanzas have survived from 1921 fundamentally unchanged, at least in this respect—for example, "The Fish," "The Monkeys," and "In the Days of Prismatic Color." If "Picking and Choosing" needed recasting, then why not "In the Days of Prismatic Color" as well? To be sure, all the lines in the final version of "Picking and Choosing" are more or less end-stopped; line ends coincide with rhetorical pauses, as is emphatically not the case with the earlier versions, and two problematic hyphenations have gone as well, a "re-/warding" and an even more awkward "ve-/ry." If literature is "a phase of life," and if that means "interpreting life as emotion," for which " 'a right good salvo of barks,' a few strong wrinkles puckering the skin between the ears, is all we ask," then an artificially imposed syllabic structure may well be an impertinence; one may argue that a certain decorum has been observed in the poem's reshaping.

But the argument seems tenuous. For one thing, the changes have been gradual, progressive, rather than all at once. "Re-/warding," for example, lasted through three reprintings, in *Observations, Selected Poems,* and *Collected Poems;* "ve-/ry," on the other hand, became "very" in *Collected Poems.* In *Poems,* the amusing humbug toward the end of the poem translated *summa diligentia*

> on the "top of a
> diligence."

In *Collected Poems,* it had become

> 'on the top of a
> diligence'.

And *Complete Poems* reports it as

> on the top of a *"diligence"*!

We are no longer being trusted to see the joke by ourselves. The poem has changed in ways other than its form. In *Poems,* Hardy was

> one man
> "interpreting life through the medium of the
> emotions."

Collected Poems changed double quotation marks to single, but *Complete Poems* gives us

> one man interpreting life as emotion,

which is not the same thing. *Poems* sees it as fact

> that James is all that has been
> said of him but is not profound;

Observations,

> that James is all that has been
> said of him if *feeling* is profound.

Selected Poems abandons italics, but *Complete Poems* abandons qualification:

> James
> is all that has been said of him.

But without that qualification, the phrase loses much of its point and all of its bite, as does

> The critic should know what he likes,

from *Complete Poems*, when measured against

> If he must give an opinion, it is permissible that the
> critic should know what he likes,

from earlier printings. The movement here seems less toward decorum than toward platitude; one may feel rather that a good form for the poem has been abandoned than that a right one has been found.

And for another thing, there is "In the Days of Prismatic Color." Here the stanzaic form of *Poems* has survived through all subsequent printings: five five-line stanzas concluded by one of four lines. Only three minor verbal changes have been made in the text,[7] and all three have been carried into *Complete Poems* from earlier revision. The only alterations of the *Collected Poems* text have been in line breaks, and these are odd by reason of their inconclusiveness. Originally, the five-line stanzas showed a syllabic pattern of thirteen in the first lines, seven in the third, eighteen in the fifth, and either eleven or twelve in the second and fourth, except that stanza two was short one syllable in the first line. The anomalous line is still anomalous in *Collected Poems*, but *Complete Poems* adjusts it by changing "varia-/tion" to "variation," picking up the extra syllable and regularizing the stanza for the first time in its history. Other similar hyphenations remain ("a-/bout," "al-/ways," and even "init-/ial"), making it difficult to detect motive for change other than a desire for stanzaic regularity; Miss Moore's dislike of hyphens[8] will not do. And yet *Complete Poems* alters the third line of the third stanza by changing "murki-/ness" to "murkiness," adding an extra syllable and creating a new anomaly, precisely the reverse of the similar revision in the second stanza. Stanzaic regularity is abandoned almost completely after stanza two. And this surely is neither decorum nor system, but whim and, as with "Poetry," a readiness to have it both ways at once.

Such inconsistences make it almost impossible to generalize meaningfully about Miss Moore's revisions, especially in their most recent stages. Some need no defense, others admit of no explanation except the impulse to tinker, or perhaps to make sacrifices. The importance of moral imperatives in Miss Moore's attitudes toward art[9] and her lifelong acceptance of orthodox Presbyterian Christianity suggest that the making of sacrifices may not be altogether metaphorical here. "If he must give an opinion, it is permissible that the critic should know what he likes," is a fine, witty, malicious epigram. But for one who, having said of poetry "I, too, dislike it," says it again "of anything mannered, dictatorial, disparaging, or calculated to reduce to the ranks what offends one," [10] there may be reasons of conscience for sacrificing witty malice in favor of the humble truism, "The critic should know what he likes," or for reducing "Poetry" to those three lines in which one's own "perfect contempt" yields to grudging humility, at whatever cost to bravura. Even tinkering may have its integrity.

To return to the 1921 *Poems* and the subsequent omissions, or sacrifices, of titles it includes, three of its poems were omitted from *Observations,* six more from *Selected Poems,* and two more from *Collected Poems,* a total of eleven. In *Complete Poems,* a twelfth is omitted, but one comes back, making the same total. And on the whole it is not easy to quarrel with Miss Moore's judgment of what should be omitted, not simply because such quarreling would be ungracious but because, measured against such performances as "Peter" or "Bird-Witted" or "What Are Years?," many, and perhaps most, of the omitted poems are of that class Auden describes, commenting on any poet's collected poems, as "the pieces he has nothing against except their lack of importance." [11] Few of Miss Moore's abandoned poems are worse than this; perhaps "He Made This Screen" comes as close as any:

> not of silver nor of coral,
> but of weatherbeaten laurel.
>
> Here, he introduced a sea
> uniform like tapestry;
>
> here, a fig-tree; there, a face;
> there, a dragon circling space—
>
> designating here, a bower;
> there, a pointed passion-flower.[12]

It is competent, and perhaps more than competent. It has remote kinship with the forging of Achilles' shield in the *Iliad*.

Not burdened with adjectives or with anything to say, it is an attractive object. The worst that can be said of it is that one cannot become very much interested in it, and the best may not be much different. Perhaps the same judgment applies to "To William Butler Yeats on Tagore":

> It is made clear by the phrase,
> even the mood—by virtue of which he says
>
> the thing he thinks—that it pays,
> to cut gems even in these conscience-less days;
>
> but the jewel that always
> outshines ordinary jewels, is your praise.

It says something about integrity, but not in a way that commands attention.

"Feed Me, Also, River God," the third never-reprinted poem from *Poems,* seems to be a different problem:

lest by diminished vitality and abated
vigilance, I become food for crocodiles—for that quicksand
of gluttony which is legion. It is there—close at hand—
  on either side
  of me. You remember the Israelites who said in pride

and stoutness of heart: "The bricks are fallen down, we will
build with hewn stone, the sycamores are cut down, we will
                                  change to
cedars"? I am not ambitious to dress stones, to renew
  forts, nor to match
  my value in action, against their ability to catch

up with arrested prosperity. I am not like
them, indefatigable, but if you are a god you will
not discriminate against me. Yet—if you may fulfil
  none but prayers dressed
  as gifts in return for your gifts—disregard the request.

Here too integrity seems to be the subject. Humble and help-less prayer for sustenance modulates into a recollection of heroic, if hubristic, resolution. (The quoted passage is from Isaiah 9:10, words that Isaiah attributes to Israel as sympto-matic of blind self-assurance.) But such recollection, however remote its object from the petitioner's circumstances, modifies her humility, and the prayer becomes conditional. The Isra-elites had pride and stoutness of heart; the petitioner has only fastidiousness and a not quite cranky insistence on candor, demanding that prayer not pretend to the status of a *quid pro quo* and putting the river god firmly in his place. Unlike the other two, this is a poem of wit. Why was it omitted? Perhaps it lacks the epigrammatic neatness of "To a Steam Roller," for example, which also appears in *Poems*; perhaps the river god needs more accounting for than the verse from Isaiah affords, though it is hard to believe that he is much more problematic than the cat in "My Apish Cousins," which survived as "The Monkeys." But perhaps the Israelites' "ability to catch/ up with arrested prosperity" came to look suspiciously like a politely anti-Semitic Anglo-Saxon stereotype, of especially questionable taste in a poem that praises fastidiousness. One of the labors in "The Labors of Hercules," first published in *The Dial* in 1922, is

> to convince snake-charming controversialists
> that one keeps on knowing
> "that the Negro is not brutal,
> that the Jew is not greedy,
> that the Oriental is not immoral,
> that the German is not a Hun."

And though "Feed Me, Also, River God" did not reappear in *Observations,* an odd sort of survival did appear both there and in *Selected Poems* in the poem entitled " 'The Bricks Are Fallen Down, We Will Build with Hewn Stones. The Syca-mores Are Cut Down, We Will Change to Cedars' ":

> In what sense shall we be able to
>   secure to ourselves peace and do as they did—
> who, when they were not able to rid
>   themselves of war, cast out fear?
>   They did not say: "We shall not be brought
>   into subjection by the naughtiness of the sea;
> though we have 'defeated ourselves with
>   false balances' and laid weapons in the scale,
> glory shall spring from in-glory; hail,
>   flood, earthquake, and famine shall
>   not intimidate us nor shake the
>   foundations of inalienable energy." [13]

It is difficult to see in this anything more reprehensible than praise of courage and distaste for bravado.

All the other poems in *Poems* survive through at least one more printing, in *Observations*; six of them were abandoned after *Observations,* as were eight others first collected in that volume. Of the six, only one, "A Talisman," seems to approach the excessive simplicities of "He Made This Screen" and "To William Butler Yeats on Tagore," and T. S. Eliot has said all that needs to be said of it in his introduction to *Selected Poems.* "To a Chameleon," the more economically titled *Observations* version of "You Are Like the Realistic Product of an Idealistic Search for Gold at the Foot of the Rainbow," reappears in *O to Be a Dragon* and later collections with lines redistributed but no verbal alterations. Two others do perhaps contain ele-ments that might seem unsatisfactory to a fastidious taste. "Diligence Is to Magic as Progress Is to Flight" has to do with the superior value of proven over unproven means toward our ends:

> With an elephant to ride upon—"with rings on her fingers and bells
> on her toes,"
>   she shall outdistance calamity anywhere she goes.
> Speed is not in her mind inseparable from carpets. Locomotion arose
>   in the shape of an elephant, she clambered up and chose
> to travel laboriously. So far as magic carpets are concerned, she
> knows
>   that although the semblance of speed may attach to scarecrows
> of aesthetic procedure, the substance of it is embodied in such of
> those
>   tough-grained animals as have outstripped man's whim to suppose
> them ephemera, and have earned that fruit of their ability to endure
> blows,
>   which dubs them prosaic necessities—not curios.

The poem may say something about Miss Moore's habitually belittling attitude toward her own work. Whether or not it is a scarecrow of esthetic procedure, a syllabic poem in English, especially of Miss Moore's emphatically unsingable kind, had hardly outstripped in 1924 man's whim to suppose it an ephemera rather than a prosaic necessity; it remains a curio, in alternating twenty- and fourteen-syllable lines, whose practice systematically denies its preachment. Such ironies are by no means ineffective; Eliot's apologetic note in "East Coker,"

> That was a way of putting it—not very satisfactory:
> A periphrastic study in a worn-out poetical fashion,[14]

makes a similar point. But a ten-line poem with all lines rhyming on a single sound is almost bound to seem labored; this one does not escape, however skillfully the rhymes have been buried in the syntax, and Miss Moore has rarely repeated the experiment.

"Reinforcements" is less eccentric and more compelling:

The vestibule to experience is not to
  be exalted into epic grandeur. These men are going
to their work with this idea, advancing like a school of fish through

still water—waiting to change the course or dismiss
  the idea of movement, till forced to. The words of the Greeks
ring in our ears, but they are vain in comparison with a sight like
                                                              this.

The pulse of intention does not move so that one
  can see it, and moral machinery is not labelled, but
the future of time is determined by the power of volition.

First printed in *The Egoist* in the summer of 1918, it has the look of a war poem, though only the timing and the title suggest as much directly. Its point is that, although mere readiness to act is never as conspicuously exciting as action, it nevertheless has a prior claim on our respect; "the power of the visible/ is the invisible," as she was to put it twenty-three years later in "He 'Digesteth Harde Yron,'" during another war. This reading of the poem—in fact, any reading of the poem—depends on a fairly arbitrary identification of "these men" and the work they are going to; without such arbitrariness, all we have is two truisms bracketing a cryptic center that, remaining cryptic, does nothing useful for the truisms. "Although prepared for an 'element of the riddle' in any poem," Miss Moore wrote later, "an even somewhat experienced person is not irked by clues to meaning." [15] In this instance, the title may have seemed an insufficient clue.

Such speculation, however, is dangerous. On the one hand, absence of clues did not lead to abandonment of the still more cryptic "In This Age of Hard Trying, Nonchalance Is Good and," which survived all the way into *Complete Poems,* unaltered except by the addition of quotation marks and two sets of notes, one in *Collected Poems* attributing its opening line to Dostoevsky and another in *Complete Poems* attributing it to Turgenev. And on the other hand, "Dock Rats" and "Radical" did not survive beyond *Observations.* "Radical" especially seems brilliantly realized, from its functionally ambiguous title, which bespeaks both carrots and revolutionaries, to its blandly ominous final aphorism:

> Tapering
> to a point, conserving everything,
>   this carrot is predestined to be thick.
>   The world is
>   but a circumstance, a mis-
>   erable corn-patch for its feet. With ambition,
>   imagination, outgrowth,
>
> nutriment,
> with everything crammed belligerent-
>   ly inside itself, its fibres breed mon-
>   opoly—
>   a tail-like, wedge-shaped engine with the
>   secret of expansion, fused with intensive heat
>   to the color of the set-
>
> ting sun and
> stiff. For the man in the straw hat, stand-
>   ing still and turning to look back at it—
>   as much as
>   to say my happiest moment has

been funereal in comparison with this, the conditions of life pre-

determined
slavery to be easy and freedom hard. For
    it? Dismiss
    agrarian lore; it tells him this:
        that which it is impossible to force, it is
        impossible to hinder.

Firm, self-assured, and odd, the poem has to do with Miss Moore's perennial themes of adaptation and endurance. Like Engels, the carrot says that the recognition of necessity is the beginning of freedom, and that it takes a carrot to know necessity. But to the man in the straw hat, incapable of the carrot's total commitment to its destiny or of cramming everything inside himself, the world is less a mere circumstance than what Keats called a vale of soul-making,[16] designed for creatures who are not predestined to be thick but achieve thickness by their difficult choices between easy slavery and hard freedom. Like the Grecian urn, the carrot has the last word; but like the urn's formulation, the carrot's is all one needs to know only if one is a carrot. Why this poem, own cousin to "Nevertheless" with that poem's exemplary strawberry and cherry, had to be omitted from *Selected Poems*, *Collected Poems*, and *Complete Poems* is a puzzle.

"Dock Rats" seems less complex, consequently less interesting, but not sufficiently so to account very satisfactorily for its abandonment.

There are human beings who seem to regard the place as craftily
    as we do—who seem to feel that it is a good place to come
    home to. On what a river; wide—twinkling like a chopped sea
                                                under some

of the finest shipping in the

world: the square-rigged four-master, the liner, the battleship, like
the two-
thirds submerged section of an iceberg; the tug—strong moving
thing,
dripping and pushing, the bell striking as it comes; the steam
yacht, lying
like a new made arrow on the

stream; the ferry-boat—a head assigned, one to each compartment,
making
a row of chessmen set for play. When the wind is from the east,
the smell is of apples; of hay, the aroma increased and decreased
suddenly as the wind changes;

of rope; of mountain leaves for florists. When it is from the west,
it is
an elixir. There is occasionally a parrakeet
arrived from Brazil, clasping and clawing; or a monkey—tail and
feet

in readiness for an over-

ture. All palms and tail; how delightful! There is the sea, moving
the bulk-
head with its horse strength; and the multiplicity of rudders
and propellers; the signals, shrill, questioning, peremptory, di-
verse;

the wharf cats and the barge dogs—it

is easy to overestimate the value of such things. One does
not live in such a place from motives of expediency
but because to one who has been accustomed to it, shipping
is the

most congenial thing in the world.

Rather in the spirit of "When I Buy Pictures," this poem fixes
upon phenomena that give pleasure in one's average moments,

though there is less concern with the spiritual forces which made them. "Radical" is a piercing glance into the life of things; "Dock Rats" is an instance of that simplicity in which, as Miss Moore has it in "People's Surroundings," one's style is not lost. If "Radical" has remote affinities with "Ode on a Grecian Urn," "Dock Rats," approaching things wholly from the outside, and content to remain so, has comparable affinities with "To Autumn."

"Is Your Town Nineveh?" and "Roses Only" lasted through *Selected Poems* but have not been reprinted since, and here again it is difficult to see why these two should have been singled out for exclusion. Like "Reinforcements," "Is Your Town Nineveh?" has a problematic center:

> Why so desolate?
>   And why multiply
>   in phantasmagoria about fishes,
>   what disgusts you? Could
>   not all personal upheaval in
>   the name of freedom, be tabood?
>
> Is it Nineveh
>   and are you Jonah
>   in the sweltering east wind of your wishes?
>   I, myself have stood
>   there by the aquarium, looking
>   at the Statue of Liberty.

In an odd way, the point here seems more elusive than in "Reinforcements," though certain things are clear enough. The location is New York's Battery Park, at the southern tip of Manhattan, until 1941 the site of the City Aquarium and still a strategic spot for observing the Statue of Liberty. Somebody addresses somebody, in fact or in imagination, not to be like Jonah, sulking outside Nineveh because God had changed his mind about destroying that city. "Phantasmagoria about fishes" suggests both Jonah remembering—and perhaps regretting?— his days in the belly of the fish, and a New Yorker biliously regarding the aquarium.

But what is the force of the question concluding stanza one? Unless it is addressed to oneself and one is prepared to regard oneself as a carrot, the question seems impertinent. But if it is addressed to oneself, if the poem is Miss Moore admonishing Miss Moore, then who is "I" in the final statement of stanza two? Or is the speaker really God, from whom no question is impertinent, ironically addressing some latter-day Jonah in the spirit of "Doest thou well to be angry?" [17] But Jonah's personal upheaval was not in the name of freedom—at least not that part of it that exposed him to a sweltering east wind [18]— and in any case, how do we understand the gesture of God's, or Miss Moore's, or someone else's standing by the aquarium and looking at the Statue of Liberty? Is it simply that one can in fact do these things without being put out of temper? A good poem always raises more questions than it answers, but a really good poem also provides answers to questions one never thought of raising; one asks for scorpions and gets bread. Randall Jarrell has observed of "In This Age of Hard Trying, Nonchalance Is Good and," "Is this an aphorism in the form of a fable, or a fable in the form of an aphorism? It doesn't matter. But how sadly and firmly and mockingly *so* it is, whatever it is; we don't need to search for an application." [19] We are not sure whether "Is Your Town Nineveh?" is *so* or not.

"Roses Only" may be; its answers, at least, are more surprising and more satisfactory:

You do not seem to realize that beauty is a liability rather than
an asset—that in view of the fact that spirit creates form we are
justified in supposing
that you must have brains. For you, a symbol of the unit, stiff
and sharp,
conscious of surpassing by dint of native superiority and liking for
everything
self-dependent, anything an

ambitious civilization might produce: for you, unaided to attempt
through sheer
reserve, to confute presumptions resulting from observation, is
idle. You cannot make us
think you a delightful happen-so. But rose, if you are brilliant, it
is not because your petals are the without-which-nothing of pre-
eminence. You would look, minus
thorns—like a what-is-this, a mere

peculiarity. They are not proof against a worm, the elements, or
mildew
but what about the predatory hand? What is brilliance without
co-ordination? Guarding the
infinitesimal pieces of your mind, compelling audience to
the remark that it is better to be forgotten than to be remembered too violently,
your thorns are the best part of you.

To be sure, there is elusiveness here as well. The notion of the rose attempting to convince us, who know better, that it has no brains does raise questions regarding the limits of explicit whimsy. Even recognizing, as one does, that Miss Moore's rose, unlike Miss Stein's, is something more than a rose—may in fact be a dumb blonde—one may find a rose with "infinitesimal pieces of . . . mind" too imaginary a garden to harbor a real toad.

And yet this conservative rose is in its way as memorable as the radical carrot, and as wittily rendered. The carrot tells us what life is; the rose, what roses are. And both, speaking from their limited perspectives, give us less than we, or they, need to know. One cannot stop a carrot from growing nor a rose from being beautiful; but the cost of remaining satisfied with such knowledge is to be a mere "wedge-shaped engine with the secret of expansion" or a thornless what-is-this, the easy victim of any predatory hand or man in a straw hat. "Roses Only" was first published in 1917 by Alfred Kreymborg in *Others: An Anthology of the New Verse*; twenty years later Miss Moore offered similar wisdom in "Bird-Witted," whose mother mockingbird knows what the rose does not—that beauty is a liability rather than an asset, that brilliance without coordination is no preservative, and that audience must sometimes be compelled to the remark that it is better to be forgotten than to be remembered too violently. And perhaps the later poem seemed an improvement—more lucid, more concrete, less acrobatically implausible.

Perhaps. But one can find such explanations under any cabbage plant, and they do not explain. "Black Earth" first appeared in *The Egoist* in 1918, and reappeared in Kreymborg's *Others for 1919*. It was reprinted in *Poems*, in *Observations*, and in *Selected Poems*. With four lines altered and the title changed to "Melancthon," it appeared again in *Collected Poems. Complete Poems* omits it.

Openly, yes,
with the naturalness
    of the hippopotamus or the alligator
    when it climbs out on the bank to experience the

sun, I do these
things which I do, which please
    no one but myself. Now I breathe and now I am sub-
    merged; the blemishes stand up and shout when the subject

in view was a
renaissance; shall I say
    the contrary? The sediment of the river which
    encrusts my joints, makes me very gray but I am used

to it, it may
remain there; do away
    with it and I am myself done away with, for the
    patina of circumstance can but enrich what was

there to begin
with. This elephant skin
    which I inhabit, fibred over like the shell of
    the coco-nut, this piece of black glass through which no light

can filter—cut
into checkers by rut
    upon rut of unpreventable experience—
    it is a manual for the peanut-tongued and the

hairy toed. Black
but beautiful, my back
    is full of the history of power. Of power? What
    is powerful and what is not? My soul shall never

be cut into
by a wooden spear; through-

out childhood to the present time, the unity of
life and death has been expressed by the circumference

described by my
trunk; nevertheless, I
        perceive feats of strength to be inexplicable after
        all; and I am on my guard; external poise, it

has its centre
well nurtured—we know
        where—in pride, but spiritual poise, it has its centre where?
        My ears are sensitized to more than the sound of

the wind. I see
and I hear, unlike the
        wandlike body of which one hears so much, which was made
        to see and not to see; to hear and not to hear;

that tree trunk without
roots, accustomed to shout
        its own thoughts to itself like a shell, maintained intact
        by who knows what strange pressure of the atmosphere; that

spiritual
brother to the coral
        plant, absorbed into which, the equable sapphire light
        becomes a nebulous green. The I of each is to

the I of each
a kind of fretful speech
        which sets a limit on itself; the elephant is?
        Black earth preceded by a tendril? It is to that

phenomenon
the above formation,
        translucent like the atmosphere—a cortex merely—
        that on which darts cannot strike decisively the first

time, a substance
needful as an instance
    of the indestructibility of matter; it
    has looked at the electricity and at the earth-

quake and it is still
here; the name means thick. Will
    depth be depth, thick skin be thick, to one who can see no
    beautiful element of unreason under it?

And what is wrong with it? Granted, it has problematic spots. I have never altogether convinced myself that I see the point of "the blemishes stand up and shout when the object/ in view was a/ renaissance," nor why the elephant's skin is a "piece of black glass," nor who "the peanut-tongued and the/ hairy toed" are.

    Stanzas fourteen and fifteen were obscure enough for Miss Moore to venture a revision for *Collected Poems*:

        the elephant is
    black earth preceded by a tendril? Compared with those

phenomena
which vacillate like a
    translucence of the atmosphere, the elephant is
    that on which darts cannot strike decisively. . . .

But apparently the increase in clarity was not enough, if in fact it was lack of clarity that led to the poem's abandonment. And it seems to me that the revision clarifies only superficially, that the phrasing is easier to follow but that it muddies the point. The point is that, to the "wandlike body . . . which was made to see and not to see," (us, surely) an elephant is—that is, appears to be—simply "black earth preceded by a tendril," a useful thing because it is tough, "thick"; and such vision is little better than blindness. The operative word is "to"; to that phenomenon (the wandlike body, the tree trunk without roots, the spiritual brother to the coral plant), it (the elephant) is the above formation (black earth preceded by a tendril). Changing "to" to "compared with" changes everything and loses a good deal of the tightly interrelated quality that the original of the revised passage has in its context. For instance, the wandlike body, once more, was made "to see and not to see"; it has a peculiar perspective; *to it*, things are and aren't visible. And again, "The I of each is to/ the I of each,/ a kind of fretful speech/ which sets a limit on itself," and an elephant is *to the other creature* a case in point. As with William Carlos Williams' red wheelbarrow, so much depends upon these delicate relationships that the risks involved in altering them are formidable.

Abandonment of this sort ought to say one of two things: either that the poem presents technical problems that cannot be resolved by revision, or that, for whatever reason, the poem's statement is no longer acceptable. Miss Moore tried revision; it evidently did not do what she wanted, and the very fact that other technical difficulties in the poem, problems of clarity and of reference, never did get revised suggests that technical clarity was not really the problem. Nor need it have been; for all its oddness and occasional slippery patches, the poem makes its statement of the elephant's eye view of things. Briefly, an elephant is an identity, inhabiting but not identical with its skin, which serves to protect what is inside it and to keep the outside out where it belongs, an enriching patina of circumstance and unpreventable experience. Thus attuned to the demarcation between inside and outside, the elephant has poise, reserve, and a sense of mystery not so clearly possessed by people, who attempt to absorb experience into themselves rather than gathering it as patina, and in the process blur everything, even elephants. Elephants see and hear; people, uncertain about insides and outsides, talk to themselves and are aware of one another not as identities to be respected as such but as irritating limitations on an otherwise unhindered flow of solipsism. To such creatures, an elephant is what it appears to be, a cortex merely, strong, thick, and durable, but otherwise of no significant interest, not even opaque; we do not know mystery even when confronted by it because, translucent like the atmosphere, it lets through what we are able to experience as light, however nebulously green. As Miss Moore put it in plain prose thirty years later, "convictions . . . are the result of experience," and "experience is almost certain to accept the fact that mystery is not just a nut which diligence can crack";[20] it had better, says "Black Earth."

And not only prose. "To a Steam Roller" was first collected in *Poems*, reappears in every subsequent collection except *A Marianne Moore Reader*, and in *Complete Poems* is identical with its 1921 version. The steam roller's failure has to do with butterflies rather than elephants, but its inability to respond significantly to identity, treating it instead as something to be used, is of a kind with the wandlike body's in "Black Earth." What Miss Moore found offensive in the one case, she continues to find offensive in the other. Granted that no two poems—certainly not these two—really say the same thing; granted also that "To a Steam Roller" has the look of being concerned with an individual while "Black Earth" comes close to being a generic indictment, or at least mockery, and as such sits oddly in company with such praise of the human as "Keeping Their World Large," "In Distrust of Merits," and "What Are Years?" But the same thing can be said of "The Monkeys," which survived with minor revision and an altered title; and in "The Pangolin," for instance, man as a species is no less firmly mocked than in "Black Earth." Why were the two finally acceptable, the third not?

The question takes one, I suspect, not to the poems but to Miss Moore, the cluster of reticences and discriminations that help to constitute an identity. And she has her own "black glass through which no light/ can filter." Even her friend William Carlos Williams has testified to her unwillingness to clarify her poems,[21] and Allen Tate detects a similar reluctance to expose herself in her whimsical rejection of Roman Catholicism on the grounds that her sins were too numerous to inflict on a confessor.[22] "Writing," Miss Moore tells us, "is an undertaking for the modest," [23] and modesty evidently precludes a parading of those reservations that have led to her persistent refashioning of her work. There are occasional notes: for example, "The five-line stanzas in my *Collected Poems* warn one to write prose or short-line verse only, since my carried-over long lines make me look like the fanciest, most witless rebel against common sense." [24] This is not true, and one cannot tell whether it is an excessive but genuine *mea culpa* regarding a formal peculiarity, or a smoke screen of some sort, a rationale for changing "Peter" and "Picking and Choosing," for example, while leaving "The Monkeys" (six-line stanzas) or "Critics and Connoisseurs" (nine-line stanzas) substantially unaltered. Such whims presumably operate in defense of something, some feeling of integrity, some "beautiful element of unreason," but it is clearly whim that operates.

Does it matter? To Miss Moore, it evidently does, but without a clearer sense than we are ever likely to get of just what it is that has troubled her in omitted and revised poems, we have little choice but to regard her tinkering as one of those things which an elephant does and which please no one but itself. Lacking that clearer sense, one may wonder whether it need matter to anyone except Miss Moore, and one need not question her genuineness or personal integrity in order to think that it matters a good deal. But it may be difficult to indicate precisely *why* it matters. Randall Jarrell gives part of the answer in his comment on the shortened version of "The Steeple-Jack" that appeared in *Collected Poems:* "The reader may feel like saying, 'Let her do as she pleases with the poem; it's hers, isn't it?' No; it's much too good a poem for that, it long ago became everybody's, and we can protest just as we could if Donatello cut off David's left leg." [25] (Incidentally, Jarrell included "Melancthon," the *Collected Poems* title of "Black Earth," in his list of Miss Moore's best poems.[26])

Jarrell's response is surely sound. And yet it is not precisely, or not simply, a matter of a poem's being too good to be altered. There are, it seems to me, at least two other elements involved. In the first place, for a poem to register itself on one's awareness as a thing, it has to have some sort of shape. This need not be an arbitrary shape, like a sonnet or a five-line syllabic stanza; it may equally well be its own uniquely organic shape, like a chestnut tree or a thumbprint or "Howl." But a poem that is subject to persistent tinkering, that appears first in strict syllabic stanzas, then as thirteen lines of freely cadenced verse, then twice in loosely syllabic stanzas, and then as three irregular lines with a long footnote, that uses double quotation marks in its first two appearances, single quotation marks in its third and fourth, and double again in the footnote to its fifth, and whose third version is identified by its author as original—such a poem is less a thing than an open-ended process; it is Polonius's cloud. Its successive revisions call attention less to the poem, which one can never grasp because it is never finished, than to the poet, who excites one's curiosity. Actually, what probably happens under such circumstances is that one really accepts that version of the poem in which it first called itself to one's attention, and writes off the others as interesting or exasperating aberrations; one can ordinarily neither entertain equally four different versions of a poem nor simply cancel earlier versions when a later appears. Clearly, a poet is under no obligation to concern himself with such problems; but a poem whose history is one of never quite finding its shape suffers because of them.

And in the second place, a volume entitled *Complete Poems* legitimately arouses certain expectations; it has an obligation to be complete, and that obligation would not be fulfilled by a volume of Eliot, say, that omitted "Marina" and "Sweeney Among the Nightingales," turned "The Love Song of J. Alfred Prufrock" into free verse, and removed part three of "The Waste Land." This is, I think, more than a prig's quibble over titles; at the risk of portentousness, it has to do with the reality of the past. Not counting anthology appearances, "Roses Only" has been printed at least four times, "Black Earth"/"Melancthon" six times, "Poetry" seven times, four of them prior to the version identified in *Complete Poems* as original; at least one German translation of "Roses Only" has been printed, in the 1954 *Gedichte: Eine Auswahl,* while "Poetry" exists in German, French, and Spanish translations, all prior to the three lines of *Complete Poems.* "The past is the present," as Miss Moore reminds us in the poem of that name, but in *Complete Poems* the past comes dangerously close to being what one wishes it had been. Confusion, though perhaps not confusion alone, is well served by a volume that, evidently intended to be definitive, fudges with history in this way.

"What she has she has tried to make perfect," wrote Wallace Stevens to Norman Holmes Pearson,[27] and again, to Barbara Church, "She is a moral force 'in light blue' at a time when moral forces of any kind are few and far between." [28] And a moral force concerned with making what she has perfect may well have small concern for mere consistency or for the convenience of readers who may expect a *Complete Poems* to be complete. W. H. Auden concludes that Miss Moore's poems "delight, not only because they are intelligent, sensitive and beautifully written, but also because they convince the reader that they have been written by someone who is personally good." [29] And he notes that she is "a pure 'Alice.' She has all the Alice qualities, the distaste for noise and excess . . . the fastidiousness . . . the love of order and precision . . . the astringent ironical sharpness. . . ." [30] Yet it was not Alice but Humpty Dumpty who said, "When *I* use a word, it means just what I choose it to mean—neither more nor less." Very possibly, as with the late egg, it may take all the king's horses and men to put Miss Moore together. But what a variorum edition it will be.

CHAPTER 4

Intelligence in Its Pure Form

The table of contents in Marianne Moore's 1967 *Complete Poems* has a degree of interest not ordinarily possessed by such documents: it indicates by its structure how she regards her work as a whole. Part I, *Collected Poems*, substantially reproduces the table of contents of that volume, with its separate subheadings for *Selected Poems, What Are Years?*, and *Nevertheless*, and for the nine poems brought together for the first time in the 1951 volume. Part II, *Later Poems*, includes separately *Like a Bulwark, O to Be a Dragon, Tell Me, Tell Me*, four hitherto uncollected poems, and nine of her translations from La Fontaine. Three facts strike one about this: first, that *Collected Poems*, or the revised version thereof, evidently has for Miss Moore an importance equaled by no other single volume; second, that within these large divisions the chronology of the separate volumes is still meaningful enough to be maintained; but, third, only up to a point, because both *Poems* and *Observations* have been allowed to slip out of the chronology, and because "The Student," for example, whose complicated history takes it back to 1932,[1] is here reassigned to *What Are Years?* (1941), where it did in fact appear as part of the separate volume, but not in the version of that book reprinted in 1951 as part of *Collected Poems*. As we noted at the end of the last chapter, Miss Moore's sense of history is selective and changeable.

Or perhaps creative. *Complete Poems* has in fact an oddly attractive wheels-within-wheels look to it. Broadly speaking, it consists of *Collected Poems* and other, later things, though "later" must occasionally be taken in a Pickwickian sense. But *Collected Poems* itself consists of *Selected Poems* and other, later things, with the same proviso. *Selected Poems* conceals its constituent elements, but it in its turn consists of thirty-five poems preserved from *Poems* and *Observations* and ten other, later things—"The Monkey Puzzle," first printed in *The Dial* in 1925, and the first nine titles in *Complete Poems,* none printed prior to 1932. *Observations* itself cannot be described in quite the same terms; it consists of twenty-one poems from *Poems,* a dozen or so others that had been printed in periodicals by the time of *Poems* but were not reprinted there, and a slightly larger number that were either published between 1921 and 1924 or that received publication for the first time in *Observations.* In each instance earlier work is consolidated, sometimes revised or deleted, and later work, sometimes embodying or suggesting new directions and altered concerns, is brought into the record.

It seems apparent that the earliest stage Miss Moore wishes to preserve of that cumulative consolidating of the past is *Selected Poems,* and I doubt that there is much difficulty in seeing why, in the light of what comes after it in *Collected Poems.* The lingering quality of *Selected Poems* might reasonably be labeled an ironic and fastidious detachment, and the difference between that and such poems of the war years

as "What Are Years?," "Nevertheless," "In Distrust of Merits,"
and " 'Keeping Their World Large' " is startling, whether one
sees it with Charles Tomlinson as a movement toward sen-
timentalizing,[2] or with Robert Penn Warren as a movement
into greatness.[3] In either case, something substantial has happened to her sense of what may appropriately go on in a poem,
something substantial enough to have bothered her considerably. Of "In Distrust of Merits," she has said, "It is sincere
but I wouldn't call it a poem. It's truthful; it is testimony—to
the fact that war is intolerable, and unjust," but it is also
"haphazard; as form, what has it? It's just a protest—disjointed,
exclamatory. Emotion overpowered me. First this thought and
then that." [4] And none of her other ventures into new territory,
if that is what they are, are as marked as this one.

Still, the pattern is visible in earlier stages as well, and if one
suspects, as I do, that Miss Moore's finest work is in those last
three sections of *Collected Poems,* it may be worthwhile to
examine the stages by which *Collected Poems* came into being,
even though the results may prove fairly inconclusive. Such an
examination may as well begin with the table of contents of
Selected Poems, which falls into four subdivisions. The first
nine titles, from "The Steeple-Jack" through "Nine Nectarines,"
are of poems first printed in book form in *Selected Poems,*
though all of the nine had appeared in periodicals from 1932
to 1934. The next thirteen, from "To a Prize Bird" through
"When I Buy Pictures," are reprinted from *Poems* and/or
Observations; with the single exception of "Peter," which had
its first publication in *Observations,* all of this group had appeared in periodicals in 1921 or earlier, thus belonging to the
era of *Poems,* and Miss Moore's including "Peter" with them

suggests that it too was written prior to 1921. The next eleven titles, from "A Grave" through "Sea Unicorns and Land Unicorns," had first appearances between July, 1921, and 1924 and had their first book publication in *Observations*, with the exception of "Those Various Scalpels," which had appeared in *Contact* for January, 1921, and in *Poems*, where it was reprinted from a still earlier appearance in the Bryn Mawr *Lantern*. Of the remaining twelve, all but the first, "The Monkey Puzzle," were collected in *Observations*, two ("To a Steam Roller" and "'He Wrote the History Book'") had appeared also in *Poems*, and three ("An Egyptian Pulled Glass Bottle in the Shape of a Fish," "To a Snail," and "Nothing Will Cure the Sick Lion but to Eat an Ape") were first printed in *Observations*. Except for those three, all had appeared in periodicals, and all but the first and last, "The Monkey Puzzle" and "Silence," had appeared from 1915 through 1917—again, in the *Poems* era, though on the whole earlier than the thirteen poems in group two. "Silence" had been printed in *The Dial* in October, 1924, and also in *Observations*; "The Monkey Puzzle" was in the same periodical for January, 1925, too late for the book.

In general these divisions are self-explanatory. The first consists of poems new in *Selected Poems*, the third of poems new in *Observations*, and the others of earlier work. But there is a small puzzle in the treatment of the earlier work; why is it divided between groups two and four rather than appearing as a single group? And, at the risk of detecting ingenuities that are not there, why is group two spliced onto, while group four is separated from, group three? "Those Various Scalpels," which did appear in *Poems* and hence seems to belong with group two, is nevertheless the second poem in group three; the two groups overlap. And "The Monkey Puzzle," strictly speaking, belongs to neither group three nor group four, which it separates in the table of contents, since it evidently was not written until after *Observations* was published. A likely explanation for the placing of this poem is that it seems to have been the last poem Miss Moore wrote before joining the staff of *The Dial*, and in fact the last poem she published until 1932; it is clearly of the *Observations* era, though just too late for inclusion therein. In any event, to go from "The Monkey Puzzle" to "Injudicious Gardening," the next poem, is to go back ten years in time, from 1925 to 1915.

As group four begins anomalously, so does it end. Of the other poems in the group that received publication prior to appearing in *Observations*, the most recent is "Sojourn in the Whale," from 1917. But "Silence," which concludes the group and also *Selected Poems*, had its first publication in *The Dial* in 1924, seven years later; it seems to belong to group three, and as a matter of fact it appears with that group in *Observations*, coming between "Marriage" and "An Octopus." [5] Chronology is being juggled, and while it would be foolish to object, one may legitimately be curious about the rationale for the juggling, particularly about the division of the early poems.

My own feeling, perhaps entirely subjective and impressionistic, is that group four includes the least successful poems of *Collected Poems*—the sports, the relative oddities, the good ideas least capable of development. Clearly, these are the wrong terms for "To a Steam Roller" and "To a Snail," except in the possible sense that epigram, when it is good, leads nowhere but to itself. And "Sojourn in the Whale," which is about

Ireland and was first printed in 1917, has a considerable degree of moral resonance if one supposes that it has to do with the Easter Rising of the preceding year. But a woman capable of sacrificing "Black Earth," "Roses Only," and "Radical" to the demands of some esthetic or moral fastidiousness is not likely to hesitate over less rigorous forms of self-criticism, such as suggesting minimal self-satisfaction regarding her earliest preserved work. Of the curious pine tree in "The Monkey Puzzle" she writes:

> One is at a loss, however, to know why it should be here,
> in this morose part of the earth—
> to account for its origin at all;
> but we prove, we do not explain our birth.

True curios in a bypath of curio-collecting, the poems in question prove that Marianne Moore began somewhere, though as with the pine tree we may be uncertain whether we are inspecting a monkey, a lemur, a tiger, a Foo dog, or a mere "interwoven somewhat" with a proportionable skeleton.

The poems in this group are for the most part epigrams on literature and life, brilliantly lucid and amusing in "To a Steam Roller," for example. Incapable of those "piercing glances into the life of things" of "When I Buy Pictures," equally incapable of the monkey puzzle's ability to discriminate among particulars ("It knows that if a nomad may have dignity,/ Gibraltar has had more"), the steam roller denies two of the primary bases of Miss Moore's art. It lacks half wit, is unable to leave well enough alone. An authentic Gradgrind reducing all particulars to that bleakly undifferentiated flatness that Gradgrinds and steam rollers live for, it has use for neither imaginary gardens nor real toads, neither butterflies nor snails; and it is hardly accident that "To a Steam Roller" faces "To a Snail" in *Complete Poems*. Steam rollers are indifferent to, snails exemplify, the principles hidden in such curious phenomena as an occipital horn. If a steam roller shares an absence of feet with snails and syllabic poems, its method of conclusions differs from theirs in not being hid. Mechanism confronts organism; triumphantly impersonal generalization ("Great thoughts," wrote Dr. Johnson, "are always general, and consist in positions not limited by exceptions, and in descriptions not descending to particulars." [6]) confronts a living particular ("If a Sparrow come before my Window," wrote Keats, "I take part in its existence and pick about the Gravel." [7]), and Miss Moore's kind of poet is here more Keatsian than Johnsonian.

But this reading is not as self-evident as it appears to be. Miss Moore's unkindest cuts are often directed at herself. She has never publicly referred to anyone but herself as "the fanciest, most witless rebel against common sense," [8] and Monroe Wheeler writes of her scrupulous and excessive self-condemnation for even minor complaints about the changes in her life and world.[9] Nothing prevents us from supposing that "To a Steam Roller" is directed to herself. Randall Jarrell's insistence that "she is *the* poet of the particular . . . and is also, in our time, *the* poet of general moral statement" [10] recognizes in her elements of both snail and steam roller, and in fact "To a Snail," in which we have both illustration and application, is to that extent the work of a steam roller, as are many of her animal poems. At the risk of pressing things too far, one may point out that in the absence of feet, "To a Steam Roller" has in its strict syllabic versification a more precise method of conclusions than does "To a Snail," in which the principle is laid down.

My point is that, as Jarrell notes, Miss Moore as poet persistently manifests certain tensions, certain opposed impulses that in large measure determine both her successes and her failures. Briefly, the impulse to generalize, to reduce particularities in the interests of the Johnsonian "great thought," is constantly involved with the counterimpulse to note particularities despite, or even because of, their refusal to lend themselves to application, to be generalized. On the one hand are such concluding formulations as

> Beauty is everlasting
> and dust is for a time ("In Distrust of Merits")

or

> Who rides on a tiger can never dismount;
> asleep on an elephant, that is repose. ("Elephants")

On the other hand is the unsummarizable "Marriage," described in the notes as "statements that took my fancy which I tried to arrange plausibly." When the one mode fails, the result is steam-roller stuffiness; when the other mode fails, the result is mere eccentricity, the accumulation of bric-a-bric or the pointlessly cryptic anecdote. Characteristically, they do not fail but help to define those tensions that make their poems objects of interest. Miss Moore's best work, perhaps like all best work, embodies a kind of dialectical tension between theoretically incompatible modes of knowledge and ideas of value.

I have said that this group contains the least successful of

Miss Moore's early poems, and so far I have spoken only of the brilliant exceptions. Of the others, my sense that they are less successful probably has to do with some collapse of the tension I have spoken of between the steam roller and the snail. Of steam rollers, she complains that the illustration is nothing without the application, but in "To Military Progress" the illustration hardly exists without the application. The poem is concerned with a Johnsonian great thought, that the idea of military progress is a revolting irony. It offers a kind of particular in the image of a headless torso attacked by crows while the torso's mind, presumably in the detached head, delightedly observes the process. But in a way the particular cannot be taken quite seriously; it is an *ad hoc* particular, made up after the fact in order to illustrate its thought, and one consequence is that there is little interesting or effective tension between the two. Mockingbirds and cats, pangolins and skunks are of interest and importance to Miss Moore first because they are what they are, and only second for the significance with which she can endow them; the head and torso of military progress have little of that first importance.

"Injudicious Gardening" is troublesome in another way. It looks and sounds like a wittily understated epigram, but it is difficult to get a clear sense that one knows what the poem is about, especially the second, concluding stanza. To speak more accurately, it is difficult to believe that the poem does only what it appears to do. As the notes indicate, Miss Moore has been reading *Letters of Robert Browning and Elizabeth Barrett*; she takes idiosyncratic and eccentric exception to something she has found there, then apologizes for intruding, on the grounds that different values sometimes conflict and that we must not quarrel about taste. It's an odd little moment of triumph in which Miss Moore, or her speaker, has and eats her cake, conducts a conversation and apologizes for conducting it. The word for it may be "frivolous"; the mouse labored and brought forth a mouse. Or the word for it may be "wit," defined by Dr. Johnson as that "which is at once natural and new, that which though not obvious is, upon its first production, acknowledged to be just." [11] The particulars in this instance are real enough,[12] but their relationship to the formulation that emerges (if it emerges) seems fortuitous, a mere occasion that really has nothing to do with yellow roses.

"An Egyptian Pulled Glass Bottle in the Shape of a Fish" convinces by its title, if by nothing else, that its particularity also is real, and it exemplifies one of Miss Moore's characteristic ways of organizing a poem. Thirst, patience, perpendicularity, a brittleness that is not brittleness but intensity, scaliness, polish, and refracted sunlight coexist in the poem not by virtue of intrinsic intellectual or emotional associations but simply because they coexist empirically in this particular object. As A. Kingsley Weatherhead observes of "An Octopus," Miss Moore's way "is to present and appreciate the details as they appear—she is not making a map, but engaging in what Ezra Pound called a 'periplum,' a voyage of discovery which gives, not a bird's-eye view but a series of images linked by the act of voyaging: 'Not as land looks on a map,' says Pound, 'but as sea bord seen by men sailing.' . . . a too exact structural control would defeat the poet's aim, which is to accommodate fragments which may perhaps give ' "piercing glances into the life of things." ' " [13] There is not much question but that this is the method of "An Egyptian Pulled Glass Bottle" as well, nor it seems to me is there much question but that the method works. A thoughtful voyage of discovery around this useful artifact enables us to accommodate fragments of perception and to enjoy a piercing glance into the nature of art, which gives us the wave's essential perpendicularity, the fish's capacity to dazzle.

The poem is hard to fault, perhaps impossible to fault on its own terms, and yet I find it hard to avoid the uncomfortable suspicion that mere size makes a difference here, that the method needs a degree of magnitude to fulfill its possibilities. This perhaps says no more than that "The Pangolin" or "Virginia Britannia" or even "The Fish" is a more ambitious performance than "An Egyptian Pulled Glass Bottle"; but I think that it also says that the method remains something of a tour de force when held to its epigrammatic possibilities. In "To a Giraffe," some forty years later than the poem under consideration, Miss Moore asks:

> If it is unpermissible, in fact fatal
> to be personal and undesirable
>
> to be literal—detrimental as well
> if the eye is not innocent—does it mean that
>
> one can live only on top leaves that are small
> reachable only by a beast that is tall?—
>
> of which the giraffe is the best example—
> the unconversational animal.

By then she had her answer: it does not mean that one can live only on top leaves that are small, and in fact it never had, as "England" or "Poetry" or "When I Buy Pictures" demonstrates. But the epigrams, less discursive and conversational than these, have consequently less capacity for rendering such concrete particularities as the cat Peter or the three young mockingbirds. Their brilliance, like the giraffe's, is special. "After all," as she concludes in "To a Giraffe,"

> consolations of the metaphysical
> can be profound. In Homer, existence
>
> is flawed; transcendence, conditional;
> "the journey from sin to redemption, perpetual."

The consolation derivable from the flawed nature of existence, its ability to express Johnsonian great thoughts but not itself to be wholly expressed therein, is Miss Moore's great subject, from the imaginary gardens with their irreducibly real toads to the Camperdown Elm, fifty years later, reminiscent of "Thanatopsis-invoking tree-loving Bryant" but itself a particular fact, "our crowning curio," with an arm-length hollowness in its torso "and six small cavities also." And it may be true that the epigrams, when they touch this subject, have to do more than epigram comfortably can.

Two other cases in point, of which it seems to me that one does and the other admirably does not lend substance to this view of Miss Moore's early epigrams, are "Nothing Will Cure the Sick Lion but to Eat an Ape" and " 'He wrote the History Book.' " The first works by a double surprise. Discovery of a hollowness that beauty cannot redeem might reasonably be expected to induce emphasis on the ugly; in this case, the poem's subject, realizing that "disproportionate satisfaction anywhere/ lacks a proportionate air," surprises us first by apparently recognizing that trap and second by falling into it backwards. It is a small moment of fine comedy, but what it does finally is to illustrate a platitude rather than present a particular. " 'He Wrote the History Book' " does both, at least with the help of its note. Like Wordsworth's "Anecdote for Fathers," which once bore the subtitle "showing how the art of lying may be taught," [14] it has to do with the sins, or at least the flawed existence, of fathers being visited on children. But again like Wordsworth, whose Leech-Gatherer was larger than any doctrine Wordsworth could derive from him, Miss Moore allows her event to retain a contingency and circumstantiality— amusement, respect, enlightenment, self-deprecation, gratitude —that particulars do and doctrines and platitudes usually do not possess.

The other poems preserved from the time of *Poems*—my second group—may or may not be on the average somewhat later than these, but they are larger, longer, less rigorously compressed. ("Poetry," in its three-line form, and "To a Prize Bird" are exceptions in *Complete Poems,* but not in *Selected Poems* when that volume first appeared or when it was revised for *Collected Poems*; in both instances "Poetry" had its twenty-nine line form and "To a Prize Bird" did not appear at all, having been abandoned after its printing in *Observations.*) In them the method described above is followed quite regularly and as a rule without the sometimes troublesome degree of selectivity, of inconsequence, or of patness visible in the epigrams. "The Fish" is a particularly serviceable case in point. Its subject is not fish but either a wave in a chasm or a chasm with a wave in it, and in either case the poem celebrates durability and life. Observation of fish, mussels, barnacles, submarine sunlight in rock crevices, all the miscellaneous observable clutter of a tidal coast, finds its point of interest in water and rock that oppose one another and, opposing, exhibit common characteristics:

> The water drives a wedge
> of iron through the iron edge
> of the cliff.

Such handling of opposites can well lead to confusion ("it is a privilege," she was to write in "The Steeple-Jack," "to see so/ much confusion"), and a rich and controlled confusion characterizes both the poem and the method. Visually speaking, barnacles encrusting the side of a submerged rock can equally well be seen as encrusting the side of the wave that submerges, as they are here, to the considerable confusion of a first reading. Submarine creatures slide in a medium of iron; fish wade; mussel shells adjust ash heaps; and we are finally unsure whether the "defiant edifice" of stanza six, which normal probability tells us is the cliff, may not be the wave that assaults it, "held up for us to see/ in its essential perpendicularity," as in "An Egyptian Pulled Glass Bottle." Visually speaking once more, "lack/ of cornice, dynamite grooves, burns, and/ hatchet strokes" may describe the surface either of a wave or of a chasm; we remember the barnacles. "The chasm side is/ dead," but "it can live/ on what cannot revive its/ youth"—the chasm side's youth? The youth of that which the chasm side can live on? Is the "it" that can live the chasm side, or the defiant edifice which may or may not be the same thing? And does it matter that what the sea grows old in has to be a chasm rather than a chasm side? Or may the sea grow old in a wave? Does the chasm side, which is dead, sum up the defiant edifice, or is it an "on the other hand" relationship?

Rocks are usually in the sea; here, the sea grows old in the rock. But through this astonishing hurly-burly of impression, the symbiotic confounding of wave and chasm, water and rock, dead, living, or merely able to live, stands as an image of man and his mortality—the flawed existence of "To a Giraffe," the mortality that is eternity in "What Are Years?" where the same image of the sea in a chasm receives its definitive, rock-crystal statement.

"With a great air of implying everything, it implies almost nothing," [15] wrote R. P. Blackmur of the abandoned poem "A Talisman," and the remark is an apt description of some of Miss Moore's more problematic poems. "In This Age of Hard Trying, Nonchalance Is Good and" may be a case in point, or it may be a mousetrap for the unwary reader. There can be no question but that it is extraordinarily cryptic; there may be a good deal of question whether it is cryptic about accidentals or essentials. We know that "The Fish" is about sea and stone; we do not have equivalent knowledge of "In This Age of Hard Trying." Bernard Engel points out that the poem depends not on a well-defined object but on an implied story,[16] and this is clearly accurate; but the story escapes us. It sounds vaguely Hesiodic or Homeric, possibly Socratic, and may well be neither. Miss Moore's note tells us that Turgenev's *Fathers and Sons* provided the phrase about the gods and clay pots,[17] but the episode in Turgenev throws little or no light on the first two stanzas, none at all on the last two. We have in fact a Poundian periplum, a voyage of discovery, around something that may not be there at all. The method of such poems is here subjected to an ultimate test of its ability to work—unless of course one has simply missed the point, the allusion that would draw together clearly the staff, the bag, the polished wedge, the conversation of five hundred years, and the privileged fool.

It is possible to regard this particular sort of crypticness as a class affliction. Writing mercilessly about Boston, Elizabeth Hardwick has described what she calls

the amateur not by choice but from some final reticence of temperament. . . . He will commit himself with a dreamy courage to whatever graces of talent he may have and live to see himself punished by the New England conscience which demands accomplishments, duties performed, responsibilities noted, and energies sensibly used. The dying will accuses and the result is a queer kind of Boston incoherence. It is literally impossible much of the time to tell what some of the most attractive men in Boston are talking about. Half-uttered witticisms, grave and fascinating obfuscations, points incredibly qualified, hesitations infinitely refined—one staggers about, charmed and confused, by the twilight.[18]

There is little evidence of a dying will about Miss Moore; as Randall Jarrell remarked, she seems representative "of a class-segment that has almost been freed either from power or from guilt." [19] And in a way Miss Hardwick's point has much in common with Miss Moore's point in her next poem, "To State-craft Embalmed," in which an emblematic ibis, that "incarnation of dead grace" and one of the very few of her animals that Miss Moore seems positively to dislike, goes

> staggering toward itself and with its bill
> attack[s] its own identity, until
>   foe seems friend and friend seems
>   foe.

This is not unlike the behavior of a Hardwick Bostonian. But it also has something in common both with the "byplay," "the feigned inconsequence of manner" of someone in whom the gods' arrogance has been transformed into "that weapon, self-protectiveness," and with Miss Moore's odd maneuverings in giving us whatever it is precisely that "In This Age of Hard Trying" holds up for inspection.

It would be interesting and perhaps revealing to know who, revolving upon the axis of his worth, "half limping and half ladyfied," is held up for inspection in "To Statecraft Embalmed." And it seems to me that it does no good to suppose that the poem's ibis is an anonymous type; like Pope's Atticus, this is portraiture, not simply formula. It differs from most of her animal poems, not in suggesting the human, but in occasionally denying the animal. Her jerboa, her mockingbirds, and the cat Peter do nothing that an animal would not presumably do; her ibis, like that other cat in "The Monkeys," does more. It winds snow silence round us; it stalks about with moribund talk; though alive, it is dumb, and, since it has been talking, "dumb" cannot mean simply speechless; it is slow to remark the steep, too strict proportion of its throne. And these failings are human, not animal, even when the animal, like this one, is also a cult object. Of the ibis, we are told that "Discreet behavior is not now the sum/ of statesmanlike good sense"; and of later statesmen ("To Statecraft Embalmed" was first printed in 1915) Miss Moore in 1937 wrote to Ezra Pound, "I dislike Eden and Baldwin as much as if I knew them personally." [20] Closer to 1915 might be Siegfried Sassoon's defunct ambassador, whose war diary (of the First World War) exhibited

> No exercise of spirit worthy of mention;
> Only a public-funeral grief-convention;
> And all the circumspection of the ages.

The visionless officialized fatuity
That once kept Europe safe for Perpetuity.[21]

"As if a death mask ever could replace/ life's faulty excellence!" As if it could! Characteristically Miss Moore's anger and contempt are more restrained, less heavy-handed than Sassoon's; her byplay, we may say, is more terrible in its effectiveness than the fiercest frontal attack. Or we may say that, pulling her crucial punches as if excessive popularity might be a pot, she throws away something that might have split the firmament.

For "Poetry" in its final form, as for embalmed statecraft, there is nothing to be said; neither an imaginary garden nor a real toad, it manages to be at once arrogant, commonplace, condescending, and pseudo-ingenuous. Its brilliant predecessor, though relegated to the status of a footnote, survives, to insist that poetry has to do with concretely realized particulars of whatever sort, in and through the realization of which we may, if we are lucky, arrive at such imaginatively apprehended moments of insight and awareness as Wordsworth experienced climbing Mt. Snowdon by night, or Keats listening to a nightingale, or Yeats visiting an elementary school classroom. Romanticism, we realize, may be astringent and self-deprecatory as well as egotistically sublime.

Judging from its title, "Pedantic Literalist" may be supposed to exemplify what "In This Age of Hard Trying" identifies as "the haggish, uncompanionable drawl/ of certitude," the operation of those "half poets" who, in the notes version of "Poetry," merely drag facts into prominence. Yet only the title suggests that the poem is about, or possibly spoken by, a pedantic literalist; it comes dangerously close to being a test of the reader's ability to second-guess its author. Prince

Rupert's drops and paper muslin ghosts, like the pedantic literalist's capacity for spontaneous response, are easily destroyed, but it is not easy to see why a white torch should be any more vulnerable than a green one. Meditative men, as distinct from men of action, may be particularly menaced by malfunctioning hearts since they tend to assume that the sedentary life imposes no strain; but why is such a heart's cordiality carved, and in what way can it be thought of as inlaid? There appears to be an unidentified and unguessable image lurking somewhere just out of sight, injecting an element of puzzle that serves no apparent purpose and that emphasizes, simply by virtue of being puzzling, details that have no occasion to receive such emphasis. Similarly the phrase "immutable production," appearing first as the last line of stanza two and repeated as the last line of the final stanza, calls attention to itself in a way whose purpose never quite comes clear. The "royal . . . production" of stanza two is a basically theatrical phrase, implying something special, a command performance, and it applies only to the way the metaphorical meditative man's heart served him, not to the nonmetaphorical pedantic literalist of the title.

It is much less clear what the echoing phrase in stanza four does imply. Primarily, it is the no-longer-spontanteous core's output, the core which does belong to the pedantic literalist and has to be distinguished from the meditative man's heart. Beyond that, the first "immutable production" has to do with the meditative man's heart before its becoming an obstruction to the motive it served; the second, with the pedantic literalist's core only after it has ceased to be spontaneous. The impression conveyed by syntax and rhetoric is that something quite precise is happening, yet one is finally not sure what that precise thing is, or even why the human failure under consideration should be identified as pedantic literalism rather than, say, sentimental egocentricity or mere failure of tact. The poem cannot quite carry its weight.

"Critics and Connoisseurs" triumphantly does, chiefly because it leaves us in no doubt regarding the phenomena it presents. Its pup, swan, and ant, like those hands, eyes, and hair in "Poetry,"

> are important not because a
> high-sounding interpretation can be put upon them but
> because they are
> useful,

and because they are very firmly there, casting shadows and reflecting light. The tension between moral generalization and observed particular,[22] absent or lopsided in "Pedantic Literalist," is here restored with a brilliance that Miss Moore herself rarely equals. Unconscious fastidiousness, exemplified in a child's important because useful efforts to teach his dog manners, provides a standard of conduct that swan and ant fail to meet—half poets, perhaps, who drag things into prominence but have no sense of the genuine; meditative men making royal productions out of their ordinary affairs. Recalling Miss Moore's reluctance to refer to her own product as poetry, we may avoid the conclusion either that unconscious fastidiousness describes her own sense of her own work or that this poem's rigorously regular, hence consciously fastidious, syllabic verse contradicts its tenor. "The deepest feeling," as she reminds us in the last poem in *Selected Poems*, "always shows itself in silence." And if art really is "feeling, modified by the writer's moral and technical insights," [23] then poetry, at least the deepest poetry, lies in an area of unconsciously fastidious silence that no written poem can do more than approach. More practical than Mallarmé, who also disliked poetry but had no Gilgamesh cat in his makeup, Miss Moore nevertheless appears to share something of his unattainable ideal of perfectly articulating the whiteness of the page.

Such an emphasis on the pristine becomes explicit in "In the Days of Prismatic Color," a poem more suggestive of John Donne in "An Anatomy of the World" than of Mallarmé. Deploring a world of sophistication, complexity, and murk, in which once-pristine particulars have lost outline and become sources of peculiar darkness, the poem celebrates but does not identify "the initial great truths" that remain no matter how many waves go over them. "Truth is no Apollo/ Belvedere, no formal thing." But the poem, especially in its earliest version,[24] provides its own wittily implicit comment, as it moves from regularly syllabic five-line stanzas, thoroughly formal things, to the articulated truth of its final stanza, whose four lines duplicate no part of that formal pattern. The manner in this instance suggests neither Donne nor Mallarmé but George Herbert, in such poems as "Deniall." And in "Peter," [25] whose unconsciously fastidious cat sees the virtue of naturalness, places no high-sounding interpretations on things, and carries nothing to the point of murkiness, only moral and technical insights need be added to have an artist.

Art and life, in fact. "Might verse not best confuse itself with fate?" Miss Moore asked in a 1960 poem, "Saint Valentine," and in these earliest preserved poems, that question, or

some variant of it, is the most persistent single motif. In
"Those Various Scalpels," it is

But why dissect destiny with instruments
   more highly specialized than components of destiny itself?

The instruments in question are sophisticated elaborations
of costume, coiffure, and mannerism by which an unnamed
woman is transformed into an artifact. In "Picking and Choosing," though "literature is a phase of life," of life interpreted
as emotion, nevertheless small dogs must be careful not to
overdo their art and hence to falsify; "only rudimentary behavior is necessary to put us on the scent." And in "England,"
which is really about America, life finds its appropriate
national expression, its art, even in America, that

grassless, linksless, languageless country in which
                                        letters are written
not in Spanish, not in Greek, not in Latin, not in shorthand,
but in plain American which cats and dogs can read!

Art, in "When I Buy Pictures," [26]

must be "lit with piercing glances into the life of things";
it must acknowledge the spiritual forces which have made it.

It gives us no death mask, but a perception of life's faulty
excellence—a child feeding a pup, Hardy interpreting life
as emotion, or an artichoke in six varieties of blue, objects
of concern for those literalists of the imagination who may,
in time, replace our mere interest in poetry with the genuine
thing.

With hindsight wisdom, one may say that the dominant
movement in *Collected Poems,* and perhaps in Miss Moore's

work as a whole, is from an attractive but sometimes dreadfully superior concern with life lived, or failing to be lived, in terms of an esthetic of naturalness, fastidiousness, and enlightened self-interest, to an often humble examination of partialities and objects of concern that have no prior obligations to principle and that are valued not because they illustrate a point but because, illustrating only themselves, they liberate emotion. The difference is that between, for example, the cat in "The Monkeys," and the pangolin; between the snail, whose economy we may admire, and the paper nautilus, carrying its eggs with arms wound around

> as if they knew love
> is the only fortress
> strong enough to trust to.

Some elements of this change are visible in the poems written after the years with *The Dial* and included in *Selected Poems*, the first nine titles in the table of contents, but in point of time priority goes to the group beginning with "A Grave" and running through "The Monkey Puzzle," all but "Those Various Scalpels" (too early) and "The Monkey Puzzle" (too late) first collected in *Observations*. Of this group, though they are perhaps less concerned with esthetics than are the earlier poems, the most conspicuous difference is in Miss Moore's experimenting with longer poems. "Novices," "Sea Unicorns and Land Unicorns," "People's Surroundings," "An Octopus," and "Marriage," especially the last two, are among her longest poems; "Marriage," approaching three hundred lines, is an outside limit, and for that reason if for no other demands attention.[27]

But something more than an increase in size is visible in these poems. The movement described above not only is not visible here but is positively contradicted by an indulgence in what may well be the least attractive of Miss Moore's possible selves, surprisingly snippy, waspish, and intolerant, and without much of the saving possibility that she is engaging in self-contemplation. Stiff with sarcasm, the first two-thirds of "Novices" is dominated by contempt for its subjects, "the good and alive young men" who do not sufficiently appreciate "the spontaneous unforced passion of the Hebrew language," forcing upon us instead "the little assumptions of the scared ego" that they regard as art, "the sort of thing that would in their judgment interest a lady," but that is simply and utterly lost, " 'split like a glass against a wall,' " in the power of the closing lines' "drama of water against rocks," the same image that gave substance and meaning to "The Fish."

The end may save the beginning, energy and sustained magnificence counterbalancing vanity and ungenerous irritation. But the ungenerosity is hard to do away with; it seems excessive, even to some extent confusing, as though contemptuous overconcern with the unfortunate novices of the title slipped over into contemptuous underconcern for the reader, who may often find it impossible to be sure what is and what is not sarcasm, or at whom it is directed. For example, of what they have written, novices are

curious to know if we do not adore each letter of the alphabet that
                    goes to make a word of it—
according to the Act of Congress, the sworn statement of the
                    treasurer and all the rest of it—
the counterpart to what we are:

stupid man; men are strong and no one pays any attention:
stupid woman; women have charm, and how annoying they can be.

The first three lines are clearly ironic mockery of the novices'
presumptuousness and vanity. But after the first colon, ironies
begin conflicting. Is the "stupid man" part of the novice's poem,
an indictment the novice is sure we will adore? Or is it the
speaker's—Miss Moore's—comment on the poem's unintended
implication: if the novice's poem is the counterpart to what
we are, and if it is as stupid as she suggests, then we are
indeed "stupid man" and "stupid woman." But only ironically,
since we know that the poem is stupid, and its novice author
does not—stupid man, who does not even understand what
he has written. Or stupid man—that is, oneself—who allows
himself to be afflicted with such claptrap.

The possibilities multiply, and in the course of that multi-
plication we may well lose our bearings, like a compass at
the magnetic pole. The irony about authors, "particularly those
that write the most," about "the supertadpoles of expression,"
pretty clearly *is* irony, but whose irony and from what perspective is not equally clear. Does "accustomed to the recurring
phosphorescence of antiquity" refer to the novices or to the
supertadpoles? Or are they the same thing? If so, and if they
are "averse to the antique," in what or whose ironic sense are
they accustomed to its recurring phosphorescence? And what is
the relationship between the young men's demonstration of
(and Miss Moore's apparent irony regarding) the assertion
"that it is not necessary to be associated with that which has
annoyed one," and Miss Moore's statement to William Carlos
Williams: "My work has come to have just one quality of
value in it: I will not touch or have to do with those things

I detest"? [28] Is Miss Moore in 1923, the year "Novices" was first printed in *The Dial*, being ironic about Miss Moore in 1920, the year Williams included her statement in his *Kora in Hell* (acquiring at thirty-three what at thirty-six she was trying to forget), but pretending to be ironic about a nameless "they," "blind to the right word, deaf to satire"?

It would be foolish to call this poem a failure; it would not be foolish to say that its excellence is of an uncomfortable sort, involving an unclarity of statement that seems to ride ultimately on an unclarity of feeling. There is something petty in it; it nurses a grievance that it cannot quite state—and I do not propose to speculate on the sources of that grievance. But it is present in this group of poems. In "To Statecraft Embalmed," again, no death mask can replace "life's faulty excellence." But in "The Labors of Hercules," one of those necessary labors is

> to teach the patron-saints-to-atheists
> that we are sick of the earth,
> sick of the pigsty, wild geese and wild men;

in "Novices," the sea, metaphor though it is, is preferred to the faulty excellence of the "good and alive young men"; and in "A Grave," the sea is just that,

> that ocean in which dropped things are bound to sink—
> in which if they turn and twist, it is neither with volition nor
> consciousness.

Death masks, of a sort, are proving attractive. "Marriage" speaks of "the fight to be affectionate"; "Novices" suggests that for Marianne Moore it may have been a real fight.

This point is worth lingering over, if only because Miss

Moore appears to have won her fight, insofar as such fights are ever concluded short of canonization or the madhouse. In "A Grave," Miss Moore registers irritation with a presumptuous sight-seer; the poem becomes a small sermon on the vanity of human presumptuousness, which is not unreasonable, but it gloats in its sermonizing over the thought of the offensive sight-seer drowned in the ocean he cannot monopolize. "The Labors of Hercules" works in the same way; it proposes admirable tasks—putting snobbery in its place, resisting demagoguery, encouraging committedness at least to one's own values, though if mules, "expressing the principle of accommodation reduced to a minimum," are good, then it is not quite easy to see what is wrong with the man who prefers not to use his piano as a "free field for etching." We are aware of an uncomfortable vituperativeness of attitude displayed toward those who must be changed, or who are simply committed to other values than those the poem advocates. Except for the mule, nothing is praised, and the mule's virtues are negative, like the sea's.

"New York" and "People's Surroundings" seem less uneasily balanced. "New York" praises; the objects of its praise—commerce, the fur trade, wilderness, eagle's down ("She has a box of wild bird feathers of all kinds wrapped in tissues and a blue-jay claw. She offered me some eagle down, which she says is getting scarcer." [29])—are American and almost, if not quite, pristine, a far cry from "the beau with the muff" and other varieties of that sophistication deplored in "In the Days of Prismatic Color" and elsewhere. Quantitatively crass and even conducive to the snobbishness that is stupidity in "The Labors of Hercules" (" 'if the fur is not finer than such as one sees others wear,/ one would rather be without it' "), these phenomena justify themselves out of Henry James by offering "accessibility to experience." "Novices," "A Grave," and "The Labors of Hercules" are based on rejections; "New York" accepts, though not indiscriminately. But a quiet and perhaps suggestive revision has taken place in "New York." Earlier printings include two lines omitted from the "It is a far cry" sentence, which originally concluded:

> and the scholastic philosophy of the wilderness
> to combat which one must stand outside and laugh
> since to go in is to be lost.

To stand outside and laugh, or to go in and be lost: "Novices" stands outside and laughs; in "What Are Years?" twenty years later, "He/ sees deep and is glad, who/ accedes to mortality"; and in that great and surprising poem "In Distrust of Merits," Miss Moore, addressing her "hate-hardened heart," accuses herself of inwardly doing nothing about "the disease, My/ Self." The formula has changed; and though "New York" is not a troubling poem in the sense or to the degree that "Novices" is, it was originally less, or differently, resolved than it is now.

"People's Surroundings" is also slightly revised, also by omission, and the omitted passage is much in the spirit of "Novices" or "The Labors of Hercules." As instances of "a mind that moves in a straight line," *Complete Poems* gives us simply, "the municipal bat roost of mosquite warfare;/ the American string quartet," which had been considerably more acidulous:

> the municipal bat-roost of mosquito warfare, concrete statuary,

medicaments for instant beauty in the hands of all,
and that live wire, the American string quartette.

Yet this poem, if it reflects the fight to be affectionate, does so in other ways than those of abandoned tonalities. People's surroundings answer our questions about the people they surround—and, by and large, relieve us of the necessity to consider the people. Style is the man, and one's style is not lost in such monastic arrangements as a deal table compact with the wall. Intensely regarded, the surfaces of such arrangements go back, revealing fundamental structures, on which the interfering fringes of expression are but a stain. The revealed structures provide a kind of ideal occupational directory—"lapidaries, silkmen, glovers, fiddlers and ballad-singers,/ sextons of churches, dyers of black cloth, hostlers and chimney-sweeps"—not people but pigeonholes into which people may be sorted. Fastidious and detached, it has nothing in common with life's faulty excellence, not even to the extent of the friend in "Snakes, Mongooses, Snake Charmers, and the Like," who stands judged as "incapable of looking at anything with a view to analysis," preferring the snake to ideas about the snake. "Distaste which takes no credit to itself is best." Perhaps; but at what cost in antiseptic detachment.

"Bowls" makes a distinction between precisionists, for whom "ancient punctilio" matters, and "citizens of Pompeii arrested in action," for whom presumably nothing matters and whose death masks register a permanent condition of crisis. Miss Moore prefers punctilio. But in this case punctilio means being ironically responsive to stupid questions. Nothing is given away; something is put in its place. And a long time later she would write of her dislike for "anything mannered, dictatorial, disparaging, or calculated to reduce to the ranks what offends one." [30]

Both "Marriage" and "An Octopus" exemplify the process celebrated in "People's Surroundings," whereby under "X-ray-like inquisitive intensity . . . surfaces go back," revealing the fundamental structure under the interfering fringes of expression. The fundamental structure of marriage not unreasonably turns out to be antithesis, a matter of "opposites/ opposed each to the other/ [but] not to unity," and thus stands revealed in paradox, irony, and contradiction, in self-indulgent masculine romanticism and in equally self-indulgent feminine evasiveness, perpetually one-upping each other in a perpetual reenactment of the third chapter of Genesis. It is an engaging and witty poem, knowledgeable about Men and Women and aware that marriage among them survives more in terms of their platitudes ("'Liberty and union/ now and forever'") than of their sophistications. But it does demand capital letters—Men and Women, not men and women, brilliantly generalized from what may well be particulars, but generalized in a way that suggests not so much marriage (with a small "m") as a comedy of manners that has Marriage as its subject. Its people are not really people, but something like *commedia dell' arte* characters or very intelligent marionettes, whose manager stands outside and laughs, finding their ultimate image not in a birth or a funeral but in a statue of Daniel Webster.

And if one is concerned with fundamental structures rather than interfering fringes of expression, such emphases are wholly fitting and proper. Ten years later, in "The Hero," she was able to say, "Where there is personal liking we go." I don't mean to suggest that in 1923, the year "Marriage" was first published, Miss Moore didn't know this or would have been surprised to hear that it had something to do with marriage. But in 1923 her sense of what consititued a fundamental structure had limited tolerance for such facts. Though committed to "the silly task/ of making people noble," she provides a view of marriage that, like the poem's metaphorical coffin, "stipulat[es] space not people." Election makes not up on such conditions, for all the statesmanship of an archaic Daniel Webster. The statesmanship of an archaic Bernard Shaw, who was also committed to the silly task of making people noble and whose Jack Tanner declared marriage popular for combining the maximum of temptation with the maximum of opportunity,[31] may also be less than complete; but, touching as it does on an aspect of marriage totally lacking in Miss Moore's poem, it may do less violence to the human basis of a human institution.

"An Octopus" is not concerned with human institutions; like the sea in "A Grave," "Novices," or "The Fish," its mountain and system of glaciers (the octopus of the title) exemplify the essential nonhumanness of the nonhuman. "No 'deliberate wide-eyed wistfulness' is here"—but there was very little of that in "Marriage" either. The mountain's animals and indigenous humans, "used to the unegoistic action of the glaciers," insist on nothing, but survive without much concern for fundamental structures or neatness of finish. Only a Greek, "enjoying mental difficulties," "distrusting what [is] back/ of what [cannot] be clearly seen,/ resolving with benevolent conclusiveness,/ 'complexities which will still be complexities as long as the world lasts' "—only a Greek, or a Marianne Moore at her most puzzlingly ironic, is likely to conclude that "relentless accuracy is the nature of this octopus/ with its capacity for fact." The mountain is, in fact, Marianne Moore writ large, with her box of wild bird feathers and a blue-jay's claw. But it is also an admiring, or at least respectful, vision of a world that is almost purely mineral in its magnificent unconcern for the life that clings to its edges, too shrunken and sandblasted to engage in the fight to be affectionate.

Deliberate wide-eyed wistfulness, of a sort, is in evidence in "Sea Unicorns and Land Unicorns"; the nonhuman mountain, with its relentless accuracy and its capacity for fact, is succeeded by the human situation of maps and myths, on and in which unicorns have their lions and land beasts their marine equivalents, existing as in "Marriage" in a kind of functional opposition:

> Thus personalities by nature much opposed
> can be combined in such a way
> that when they do agree, their unanimity is great.

They agree for the cartographers of 1539, for the makers of Elizabethan embroideries, and for Sir John Hawkins, who found unicorns and deduced lions in the forests of Florida—a real garden with imaginary toads in it. But their agreement is less a fundamental structure ("People's Surroundings") than it is an imperishable wish ("Armor's Undermining Modesty"), however qualified by Miss Moore's cool and skeptical irony ("this feat which, like Herodotus,/ I have not seen except in pictures"). Like Will Rogers, she knows only what she sees in the papers; it is, in fact, odd how carefully she assures us that the affectionate myth with which the poem ends really is a myth. It may be even odder that it is one of the earliest instances of a surviving Marianne Moore poem in which such affection operates overtly, even in this carefully circumscribed fashion. The poem was first printed in the fall of 1924, and except for "An Octopus," first printed in December of that year, and "The Monkey Puzzle," of January, 1925, it was the last poem she published until 1932. "The Monkey Puzzle" takes us back to structures:

This porcupine-quilled, complicated starkness—
this is beauty—"a certain proportion in the skeleton which gives the
best results."

But "The Steeple-Jack" and "The Hero" have to do with people; and such animals as the jerboa, the tuatera, and the frigate pelican, though never quite anthropomorphic and never mere teddy bears, are objects of an unapologetic liking. Fastidiousness, conscious or unconscious, has its cost, and it seems reasonble to wonder whether part of that cost may have been the seven years of silence after 1925, only three of which were devoted to editing *The Dial*. Like the snake of "Snakes, Mongooses, Snake Charmers, and the Like," those years may suggest that "when intelligence in its pure form/ has embarked on a train of thought which is unproductive, it will come back," and that the return may be difficult.

"Intelligence in its pure form": one of the peculiarities of editing is that, though intelligence matters and may matter a great deal, it matters in something other than its pure form. Relentless accuracy may have its place, but no glacier ever conducted the affairs of a distinguished literary periodical. Editors must, while glaciers need not, deal in some mutual fashion with people and their concerns. William Wasserstrom writes of her un-glacier-like insistence that *The Dial*, under her editorship, "connect high art with the general interest," [32] the interests of people who read. And the work delighted her, as we have seen;[33] the article on *The Dial* that she included in *Predilections*, the closest thing in the book to a piece of personal reminiscence, suggests that the magazine, its office, and its people provided her with something to belong to, a place to live. She writes of "the start of pleasure with which I came on [D. H. Lawrence's] evocation of violets, in the introduction to his *Pansies*: 'Pensées, like pansies, have their roots in the earth . . .'," [34] and her own clinging to the past (eagle's down, a blue-jay's claw, a brick with a cat's paw-print in it) suggests that she had need of such roots herself. *The Dial* provided them:

I think of the compacted pleasantness of those days at 152 West Thirteenth Street, of the three-story brick building with carpeted stairs, fireplace and white-mantelpiece rooms, business office in the first story front parlor, and in gold-leaf block letters, THE DIAL, on the windows to the right of the brownstone steps leading to the front door. There was the flower-crier in summer, with his slowly moving wagon of pansies, petunias, ageratum; or a man with straw-*ber*-ies for sale; or a certain fishman with pushcart-scales, and staccato refrain so unvaryingly imperative, summer or winter, that Kenneth Burke's parenthetic remark comes back to me—"I think if he stopped to sell a fish my heart would skip a beat." [35]

"We weren't in captivity to anything," [36] she writes of *The Dial*'s staff, and in the same context, "I feel that I would not be worth a button if not grateful to be preserved from myself." [37] Something of this sort—preservation from herself, from mere crotchets and eccentricities—appears to have happened during and after the years on *The Dial*; the difference

is roughly speaking that between a concern for people's surroundings and a concern for those arrangements in which

> The hero, the student,
> the steeple jack, each in his way,
> is at home. ("The Steeple-Jack")

The merely human has become possible.

CHAPTER 5

The Other Voice

Some sort of difficulty has attended "The Steeple-Jack" and its related poems from the beginning. "The Steeple-Jack" was a seventy-eight-line poem when it first appeared in *Poetry* for June, 1932, Miss Moore's first published poem since January, 1925. As reprinted in *Selected Poems*, it had seventy-two lines; in *Collected Poems*, forty-five lines; in *A Marianne Moore Reader*, seventy-eight lines again, almost but not quite identical with the 1932 version, and bearing the misleading note "Revised, 1961"; and in *Complete Poems* it again has seventy-eight lines, slightly different from either of the other seventy-eight-line versions and retaining the note. Again, as we have seen,[1] in 1932 "The Steeple-Jack," "The Student," and "The Hero," in that order, formed a kind of tryptich with the collective title "Part of a Novel, Part of a Poem, Part of a Play." In *Selected Poems*, the collective title was kept, but "The Student" was omitted. In 1941, "The Student" was printed separately in *Furioso* and included in *What Are Years?* In *Collected Poems*, "The Steeple-Jack" and "The Hero" are separate poems with no common title, and "The Student" is once more omitted, appearing neither in its original setting nor in the version of *What Are Years?* that *Collected Poems* includes. But in *Complete Poems* it reappears as part of *What Are Years?* very substantially revised from its first version.

The breaking up of "Part of a Novel, Part of a Poem, Part of a Play" may well have come from a recognition that its apparent unity was on the whole specious, rigged, a too-insistent determination to suggest a fundamental structure that was not really there. There is a student in "The Steeple-Jack," to be sure, a "college student named Ambrose," but he has only verbal and occupational connection with the poem "The Student." And though the student in the latter poem is an Emersonian hero, his connection with the poem "The Hero" is no more substantial than with, for example, "The Frigate Pelican." Abandonment of the tryptich seems abandonment of a puzzle that, once solved, proved to have no real function. Miss Moore's only other attempt at such labeled groupings of poems appears in *The Pangolin* (1936), where the collective title "The Old Dominion" includes "Virginia Britannia," "Bird-Witted," "Half-Deity," and "Smooth Gnarled Crape Myrtle," and is abandoned after its single appearance, though the four separate poems were reprinted in *What Are Years?* It may be worth remembering too that Eliot, Yeats, and Auden had all been experimenting with ways of putting together separate poems into larger structures—"The Hollow Man" in 1925, "A Man Young and Old" in 1927, "Ash Wednesday" and "Words for Music Perhaps" in 1930, "The Orators" in 1932. In any case, Miss Moore's visible worrying over these three poems has about it something of the uncertainty of a new start in a not altogether clear direction.

There is, however, little uncertainty in the texture of the individual poems from "The Steeple-Jack" through "Nine Nec-

tarines." Perhaps only a jaundiced eye will detect in Miss
Moore's poems of the 1920s a loss of momentum, a tendency
to become more and more special, defensive, and somehow
lost; but even a jaundiced eye would be hard put to find such
qualities in the poems of the early 1930s. They have in some
fashion come to terms with the necessities of ordinary life, no
longer finding themselves in contemplation of ocean and glaciers, the vast and the inorganic. Even "the boundless sand,/ the
stupendous sandspout" in "The Jerboa" is not so much a mere
surrounding, a final judgment, or a bleak object of contemplation as it is a place to live.

Such places are much in evidence in these poems, from the
town that "Dürer would have seen a reason for living/ in," in
"The Steeple-Jack," to the frigate pelican asleep in its mangrove
swamp. The steeple-jack's town is exuberantly full of visually
exciting things, though eight stranded whales may seem excessive; Dürer made a trip to Zeeland from Antwerp in the
hope of seeing only one.[2] But stranded whales, a twenty-five-
pound lobster, the "whirlwind fife-and-drum of the storm"—all
that confusion that it is a privilege to see so much of—are
capped and transformed by a profusion of native flora that,
seemingly tropical in its abundance, turns out to be a dooryard
garden. Its cobras are cats; its ring lizards, newts; its exoticism,
domesticity; and its high adventure ("he might be part of a
novel"), routine upkeep. But routine upkeep of a place to live
in has its dignity, contributing to what the college student
named Ambrose perceives as "an elegance of which/ the source
is not bravado" (twenty-five-pound lobsters, quantities of
whales that "ambition [might] buy or take away") but rather
a kind of human functionalism or functional humanism, with

room for heroes, who are, students, who know, and steeple-jacks, who do. Danger may be present in such a world; steeple-jacks may fall, as may the spire on which they work, its pitch not true. But the subtler dangers of preferring oceans and glaciers to the things of man,

> the tired
> moment of danger that lays on heart and lungs the
> weight of the python that crushes to powder ("The Frigate
> Pelican"),

seem to be under control here.

Such preferences may or may not be among those things that the hero, in the next poem, has let go and does not covet. At any rate, what makes him a hero is his capacity for staying human in spite of the lively temptation to become either a schizoid or an *Übermensch*, hiding from life and its faulty excellence or holding himself superior to it. He has in fact won the fight to be affectionate, or at least tolerant,

> looking
> upon a fellow creature's error with the
> feelings of a mother—a
> woman or a cat.

And this is a long way from the passionate dislike of "Novices" or "The Labors of Hercules," or even from that "distaste which takes no credit to itself" of "Snakes, Mongooses, Snake Charmers, and the Like." It comes closer to Wallace Stevens'

> central man, the human globe, responsive
> As a mirror with a voice, the man of glass,
> Who in a million diamonds sums us up,

in "Asides on the Oboe," [3] though if there is a question of resemblance between Stevens' man of glass and Miss Moore's "rock/ crystal thing to see," Miss Moore has priority of publication.

"Willingness to baffle the crass reader sometimes baffles the right one," [4] wrote Miss Moore in reviewing *Parts of a World,* the Stevens volume that contains "Asides on the Oboe," and "Wallace Stevens protects himself so well against profanation that one does not instantly see the force of what he is saying." [5] Readers of Miss Moore need not go to Stevens to find such problems. Does "He's not out/ seeing a sight but the rock/ crystal thing to see" in "The Hero" mean "He's not out seeing a sight; he's out seeing the rock crystal thing to see," as Bernard Engel suggests,[6] or "He's not out seeing a sight; he's the rock crystal thing to see"? I take it to mean the latter, that he himself is

> the startling El Greco
> brimming with inner light—that
> covets nothing that it has let go.

It is the difference between seeing reality, as Engel understands it, and being reality, an imperfect anticipation of the mortality that is eternity in "What Are Years?" In the later poem,

> He
> sees deep and is glad, who
>   accedes to mortality
> and in his imprisonment rises
> upon himself as
> the sea in a chasm, struggling to be
> free and unable to be. . . .

The hero, coveting nothing that he has let go and to that degree a free creature, is an easier, more wistful image than this, easier in the sense that certain elements of difficulty in the human situation are not so much confronted as eliminated; but it is of the same sort, a serious, open-eyed celebration of the imperfect human creature. The sometimes caustic, sometimes intolerant brilliance of the earlier epigrammatic work (and even "Poetry" exhibits this) is giving way to something like a sense of wonder and of love.

Obliquely, however. Thirty-five years later she would conclude "Love in America" explicitly and in italics, with echoes of Molly Bloom:

> Whatever it is, let it be without affectation.
> Yes, yes, yes, *yes*.

In the early thirties, she was more circuitous, more reserved; yet "The Jerboa" and "The Plumet Basilisk," whatever else they are, are poems of affection, almost without affectation. Compared with the excesses, the ingenious vulgarities of Roman and Egyptian sophisticates, the jerboa's minimal requirements—"no water, no palm trees, no ivory bed"—make it possible to appreciate him for himself. Like the hero, he covets nothing that he has let go; he lives in, not on, his world, its rock crystal thing to see, lovely, tough, and at home. And what of Jacob, who appears in the second stanza of the second part of the poem? Bernard Engel sees him as contrasted with the jerboa: "The man Jacob was led by a mirage to see a ladder to heaven; but the jerboa's perceptions are not mistaken." [7] A. Kingsley Weatherhead sees him as like the jerboa, a contrast to Romans and Egyptians: "Jacob has an immediate grasp on reality." [8]

Perhaps the point is that Jacob's vision, "the translucent

mistake/ of the desert," is in either case his human distinction, that which he cannot let go whether it be supreme illusion or supreme reality. It seems to me, in fact, that the poem works largely in terms of a kind of polarity between the perfectly adapted jerboa, for whom being at home means feeling neither lack nor superfluity, and the more problematic human creature, for whom excess (the Egyptians and Romans) or asceticism (Jacob), expressing aspiration, is a condition of his being at home in anything. "The Jerboa" is an affectionate poem, but its affection, divided as it is between man and mouse, is of different kinds. As Roy Harvey Pearce shrewdly observes, "These poems are so composed as to make for the observation of an aspect of humanity which is prefigured, and no more than that, in something non-human. Observation becomes a means to, not a mode of, insight." [9]

"The Plumet Basilisk" is either less complex or more oblique. On the one hand, people play a less substantial role than in "The Jerboa." There is no ambiguous Jacob here; all, or almost all, our attention is directed to creatures, not men, and like the jerboa they are admirable in their creaturely way. But here too observation may be a means to rather than simply a mode of insight, and the insight is human, with respect both to its origin and its object. "Mythology's wish/ to be interchangeably man and fish"—like Jacob, "part terrestrial,/ and part celestial"—reflects human aspiration, not animal adaptation, as do the poem's persistent mythological and historical echoes of Inca rites, the nine sons of true dragons, and the treasures the Spaniards missed. The basilisk's transformation from something "stiff/ and somewhat heavy, like fresh putty on the hand," into a

        nervous naked sword on little feet, with threefold
    separate flame above the hilt, inhabiting
        fire eating into air,

presents the basilisk as fine; but the human consciousness, the "imperishable wish" of "Armor's Undermining Modesty," that sees and is prefigured in that transformation, may be even finer.

"Camellia Sabina" and "No Swan So Fine" also deal with such transformations, but more uncomfortably. Both have to do with art, literally or figuratively, and what it does to life. In "No Swan So Fine" Miss Moore approaches Keats in "Ode on a Grecian Urn"; china flowers and swan on the Louis Fifteenth candelabrum are as good as new, but Louis Fifteenth is not. Like Yeats's golden bird, the swan's fineness depends on that difference. Such creatures are released from the struggle to be free and the inability to be so, of "What Are Years?" But that release makes them objects of irony: "As if a death mask ever could replace/ life's faulty excellence!" Art transforms, but the result of the transformation is a dead object; it is the process and the motive, "the imperishable wish," that count, not the thing made as a result of that process. It is perhaps no accident that Miss Moore characteristically deprecates her own work as something other than poetry, that "When I Buy Pictures" should value not the thing made but the "spiritual forces which have made it," or that the most deeply felt and moving item in *Predilections*, the final essay in the book, is a review of "the autobiographic miniature entitled *Pages of My Life*," [10] by Anna Pavlova, whose art was all in the doing, not in the thing done.

"No Swan So Fine" remains unspoken in its final irony—so unspoken, in fact, that any particular reading of the poem depends more on the sense of probabilities one brings to it than on the poem itself. How does one *know* that the expressed preference for china swans over real ones is an irony? And there seems no clear answer. "Camellia Sabina" seems clearer, though in a way it obscures the issue even more by introducing finer distinctions. In broad terms, the poem is concerned with the natural and the useful versus the artificial, and it prefers the former, at least theoretically. Artificiality reveals itself in a bottled preserve of grafted plums, in elaborately cultivated greenhouse camellias, and in the making, selection, and documentation of the various Bordeaux; natural utility, in a grape grown for the table rather than for wine, and in a mouse in a vineyard. The one results in absurdity (scentless nosegays, heaviness of soul, and a great deal of fuss), the other in pleasure and the maintenance of life. But the equation does not really work out. There is a great deal of fuss devoted even to the grapes grown to eat, as Miss Moore makes clear both in her note and in the text itself, specifying as it does the process of removing—"pluck[ing] delicately off"—those grapes that do not mature, an operation that is functional only in an esthetic sense. Further, the food grape is not simply natural; we are reminded emphatically that it is " 'born of nature and of art,' " and in this respect it cannot be distinguished from the pampered camellia except perhaps in degree. And if the busy-busy of the wine historians approaches absurdity from one direction, the whimsy about "Tom/ Thumb, the cavalry cadet, on his Italian upland/ meadow mouse" approaches it from another.

Theoretically, of course, the position is clear; fuss is worthwhile when it contributes to a useful end, and this defines good art. But as she put it later, "Poetry is the Mogul's dream: to be intensively toiling at what is a pleasure," [11] and the two criteria, pleasure and utility (more accurately, perhaps, pleasure with a utilitarian end in view and pleasure for its own sake) don't really settle the issue between them in "Camellia Sabina," as they might have earlier. There is a world of difference between the delighted amusement with which Miss Moore gives us rules for growing camellias ("Mistakes are irreparable") and the sarcasm of "Novices." It is human to make things, to take pains; "Whatever you do," she advised adolescents in 1958, "put all you have into it," [12] and her own admitted passion for bric-a-brac suggests that uselessness bothers her less than made things attract her. ("Miss Moore's apartment is the apotheosis of snugness; indeed it is snug almost to the point of restricting free movement, owing to a vast collection of miscellaneous objects she has amassed over the years. 'I suppose my life is made happier by hoarding these things,' Miss Moore says apologetically." [13]) In this instance, at least, art—the poem—is the conflict of mutually exclusive varieties of esthetic Puritanism, the one declaring that only a suitable product can justify the process of its making, the other that enthusiasm and discipline in the work of making transcend any, or no, product they might make. And in either case, the dynamic element in the making, transforming process is human aspiration.

Life, utility, and the beautifully useless ("it is a privilege to see so/ much confusion") are celebrated more or less in turn in "The Frigate Pelican," "The Buffalo," and "Nine Nectarines." The pelican gives us an explicit instance of art as process rather than production of objects; he is all performance, "a marvel of grace" even when stealing fish from other birds. The objects he makes are nothing, his nest a mere collection of "sticks for the swan's-down dress/ of his child to rest upon," but they serve to maintain life, as do his unconcern for the rising moon, his instinctive ability to "foil the tired/ moment of danger," and his subordination of his presumably idiosyncratic self "in the height and in the majestic/ display of his art." "If I do well I am blessed," says the pelican, and he can hardly help doing well.[14]

Much the same thing is true in "The Buffalo," whose subject is less obviously beautiful in his behavior than is the pelican but has a larger capacity for useful symbiotic relationships with the human world—carrying the Buddha, defending against tigers, or merely doing a day's work. This adaptability to the human, without compromising his buffalo nature, gives him an excellence that bears comparison with "any/ of ox ancestry," and especially, we gather, with those bred just for human purposes—again, Miss Moore's odd and inconsistent disapproval of things not "natural," matched in "Nine Nectarines" by her equal fondness for things made and imagined. Here, the nectarines may or may not be manmade hybrids, artifices; but pictures in books, painted plates, the peach *Yu* which "eaten in time prevents death," and the

> nectarine-loving kylin
> of pony appearance—the long-
> tailed or the tailless
> small cinnamon-brown, common
> camel-haired unicorn

quite clearly are. In fact, painted nectarines seem preferable to real ones, especially as food for unicorns. "A Chinese 'understands/ the spirit of the wilderness,'" embodying it in the enameled porcelain masterpiece he has imagined, and it is at least consistent to conclude that the wilderness whose spirit he understands and constructs masterpieces from is the artifice-making, transforming human imagination, which can be both a glory and an object of amused affection.

These fine poems, it seems to me, give hindsight wisdom the basis for understanding where Miss Moore's "other voice," [15] in Robert Penn Warren's phrase for it, came from. The particular occasion for that other voice seems quite clearly to have been the Second World War. "What Are Years?" and "The Paper Nautilus" (originally entitled "A Glass-Ribbed Nest"), the first and the last poems in the 1941 *What Are Years?*, were first published in *The Kenyon Review* in the summer of 1940 and were reprinted the following year in Oscar Williams's *New Poems 1940* with such other poems of the time as Muriel Rukeyser's "The Rotten Lake Elegy," Frederic Prokosch's "War of Nerves," Robinson Jeffers' "The Bloody Sire," and Auden's "September 1, 1939" and "In Memory of W. B. Yeats." Williams' emphasis in his anthology was on "other voices," voices speaking with "a new vitality, a kinship with reality, a concern with an answer in a world reeling with questions," [16] voices that were "representative of what the poets have felt living so close to what may be civilization's greatest crisis." [17]

What Marianne Moore felt under such circumstances, and reported with remarkable explicitness, was the reality of courage and the necessity for love. *What Are Years?* moves from its opening celebration of the one to its closing insistence on the other, and the dates of first publication for the various poems in the collection indicate that these poles really are poles rather than accidents of chronology. "Four Quartz Crystal Clocks" originally appeared with "What Are Years?" and "A Glass-

Ribbed Nest" in *The Kenyon Review*, but clearly lacks the other poems' moral centrality and is located accordingly. "Rigorists," "Light Is Speech," "He 'Digesteth Harde Yron,'" and "Spenser's Ireland" were all published later in 1940 or in 1941, but are grouped with other poems from 1935 and 1936 and, in one case ("The Student"), 1932. "The Pangolin," coming between two 1940 poems, goes back itself to 1936.[18] *What Are Years?* is an organized body of work, and its objective is the affirming of values.

"You must not be surprised," writes Auden of the poet's moral affirmations, "if he should have nothing but platitudes to say; firstly because he will always find it hard to believe that a poem needs expounding, and secondly because he doesn't consider poetry quite that important." And though the context of his observation is general, he concludes, "any poet, I believe, will echo Miss Marianne Moore's words: '*I, too, dislike it.*'"[19] Certainly one can say that the values Miss Moore affirms in these poems—courage, love, humility, patience—are the stuff of platitude, like Auden's "You shall love your crooked neighbor/ With your crooked heart,"[20] or for that matter Dante's "In la sua voluntade e nostra pace." When Miss Moore's moral affirmations startle us, it is never by virtue of their exoticism, like those eggs laid by tigers for which Dylan Thomas somewhere confessed to an early love. But startle us they sometimes do, not just by their energy and wit (this at least the earlier work had prepared us for), but by their quiet intensity.

"What Are Years?" praises courage in such terms. Its opening question seems to be rhetorical; when all are equally naked and unsafe, then the personal questions of guilt and innocence seem largely beside the point. The next question is a real question, or at least a real expression of wonder—not "what is?," a mere problem of definition, but "whence is?," how did it get here, since here it is, at once an anomaly and an example. The answer echoes "The Hero," whose subject is as scared and reluctant as the rest of us but acts in spite of it all, brimming with inner light. So here, acceding to mortality ("accede" carries overtones both of surrender and of attainment) is a source of vision, gladness, and continuity as well as defeat, which under such circumstances may be tragic triumph—not lowly satisfaction, but the purity of joy. This may suggest the later Yeats, of "Lapis Lazuli" or "The Gyres" ("Hector is dead and there's a light in Troy;/ We that look on but laugh in tragic joy." [21]) but it seems to me to be much closer in spirit to the Wordsworth of about 1807, in such poems as "Elegiac Stanzas, suggested by a Picture of Peele Castle, in a Storm, painted by Sir George Beaumont," and "Ode: Intimations of Immortality from Recollections of Early Childhood."

Miss Moore gives us no sense of a lost power, as does Wordsworth, and she is not prepared, as Wordsworth is, to base her affirmation on details of personal crisis. But the mortality that is eternity, that achieves joy by its capacity to endure misfortune, even death, has kinship with that humanizing of his soul that Wordsworth experienced as a result of his brother's drowning; it echoes Wordsworth's welcome to "fortitude and patient cheer," the joy he recognized in remembering his own earlier capacity for "obstinate questionings/ Of sense and outward things," the "soothing thoughts that spring/ Out of human suffering," and those other thoughts "that do often lie too deep for tears" and that, as Lionel Trilling has pointed out, suggest an attempt on Wordsworth's part to move from "the characteristic mode of his poetry, the mode that Keats called the 'egotistical sublime,' and a dedication to the mode of tragedy." [22] So with Miss Moore the movement is away from a vision that, brilliant, idiosyncratic, eccentric, affords private insight into that which one stands apart from— "piercing glances into the life of things," as she has it in "When I Buy Pictures," enjoyed by one who "stand[s] aside and laugh[s]," as in the unrevised version of "New York," both poems of 1921; we may compare Wordsworth's "we see into the life of things," in "Tintern Abbey," and his uncomfortable feeling of not being able to listen to the leech-gatherer's responses in "Resolution and Independence," of defensively holding himself apart. "What Are Years?" may perhaps be described as Miss Moore's "Character of the Happy Warrior."

Not all the poems in *What Are Years?* are as uncompromisingly human-centered as the title poem. "Four Quartz Crystal Clocks" praises precision, finding its images in the inorganic world of the behavior of crystals and the measurement of time, and though it is concerned with truth (punctuality may be regarded as a humble microcosm of larger forms of integrity), its tone of cool superiority, reminiscent of "Those Various Scalpels," is not that of one who has irrevocably acceded to mortality. "Rigorists" embodies this imperfect commitment in an oddly imperfect poem. Like the jerboa, the Lapland reindeer is admirably adapted to its environment; almost as rigorously functional as a quartz crystal, it is tough and beautiful and eaten by Eskimos, who owe their lives to the man who first imported it. One is not sure how to take hold of the poem. Is it about reindeer, who need nothing men can give them? Or is it about Eskimos, who need reindeer? Or is it about Sheldon Jackson, who sees deep into both the beauty of reindeer and the problems of Eskimos, who accedes to the mortal necessity of choosing, and who transcends both innocence and guilt in his choice of the human? The latter reading seems to account for the poem more satisfactorily than do the others but the accelerating and understated changes of focus by which we pass from sight-seeing to hero-seeing ("He's not out/ seeing a sight but the rock/ crystal thing to see") may leave one with a sense of something incompletely resolved, something painful behind the poem that is not being permitted to appear. Some sort of adjustment between the reindeer as an object of affectionate admiration and the reindeer as something to eat has not taken place except insofar as we can assume such an adjustment as part of the battle that Sheldon Jackson won. We are allowed to feel that Eskimos don't really eat reindeer, or at least that, like Housman's infant child, the reindeer are not aware they have been eaten. " 'Man's/ wolf to man' and we devour/ ourselves," she would write three years later in "In Distrust of Merits," appalled at what she knew yet not denying the fineness implicit in it. But in 1940, reticence and insight are still at some measure of cross purposes.

Cross purposes are less in evidence in the other poems of the volume. Courage and integrity are praised, in birds, men, and nations; "The power of the visible/ is the invisible," she reminds us in speaking of ostriches ("He 'Digesteth Harde Yron' "), and the principle applies equally to France under Nazi occupation ("Light Is Speech"), to the student under his voluntary discipline ("The Student"), and to the mother mockingbird defending her fledglings ("Bird-Witted"). *What*

Are Years? is a book about heroes, in their various degrees and under the terms established at the outset, the accession to mortality. Even the solitary cardinal of "Smooth Gnarled Crape Myrtle" has acceded sufficiently to the real conditions of existence to deny those sentimental falsifications ("artifice") with which we conceal from ourselves our essential solitude and vulnerability. The same point is made in a more complicated way in "Spenser's Ireland," in which illusions of racial pride and purity, of personal independence, and of national characteristics, even when seemingly endorsed by genuine creativity, vanish when confronted by the mortal creature they are intended to convince:

> The Irish say your trouble is their
> trouble and your
> > joy their joy? I wish
> I could believe it;
> I am troubled, I'm dissatisfied, I'm Irish.

"Virginia Britannia" seems more elaborate than any of these. A powerfully moving, elegiac poem, it has a sense of place about it that is without precedent in Miss Moore's work, suggestive of Coleridge's conversation poems or Eliot's quartets. Contrasts flicker through it: Colonial past and tourist's present, settlers and Indians, a carefully achieved "almost English green" and "what the colonists/ found here," an Indian girl and an English girl, a great sinner and a cocky republic, elaborate hybrid pansies and skeptically practical mockingbirds, the hedge sparrow, "unable to suppress/ his satisfaction in man's trustworthy nearness," and the men who took what they pleased, none of them "a synonym for mercy." Its characteristic strategy is to hold up something that man, particularly white European man, has made of himself and his surroundings in oblique confrontation with something indigenous—a zigzagging butterfly, a deer's-fur crown, native birds and flowers, a pet raccoon or a cotton-mouth snake. These confrontations are not rigged; Miss Moore does not load her dice. In spite of human arrogance and greed ("Like strangler figs choking/ a banyan"), the hedge sparrow's "ecstatic burst of joy" at the proximity of people weights the balance in favor of mortality. The poem closes in a superbly controlled formality, moving from the hedge sparrow's benediction to the darkening outline of foliage seen against a sunset, the indigenous live oak and the "agèd English hackberry" losing their separate identities, becoming "part of the ground" for clouds that,

> expanding above
> the town's assertiveness, dwarf it, dwarf arrogance
> that can misunderstand
> importance; and
> are to the child an intimation of what glory is.

Miss Moore's most Wordsworthian line brings the poem back, with grace and firmness, from the contemplation of vastness to the human world of "What Are Years?" If the latter poem is her "Character of the Happy Warrior," this perhaps is her "Lycidas." It is surely one of our great poems.

"To explain grace requires/ a curious hand," we are reminded in "The Pangolin," and the ambiguities of the word "grace" help to account for the difference between this and Miss Moore's other animal poems, as well as for the fineness of "Virginia Britannia." The word, or a variant thereof ("graceful," "graced") appears seven times in "The Pangolin"; more accurately, it occurs seven times in the first six of the poem's nine stanzas. The first five stanzas (three "graces") are about pangolins, their structure, habits, and graceful adaptation to their world; stanza six (four "graces") is a meditation on grace, deliberately confounding its esthetic with its theological sense and turning from the live animals of the opening stanzas to stone animals carved on cathedrals by live people, recipients of grace in one sense who render it in another sense in enduring art; and the last three stanzas (no "graces") directly exhibit the graceless recipient and source of grace, "Bedizened or stark/ naked, man, the self, the being we call human,"

> struggling to be
> free and unable to be,
> in its surrendering
> find[ing] its continuing.

This movement within the poem is significant; though it is probably safe to say that all of her animal poems are really and finally concerned with man, it is clear that none of them make that concern as explicit or as extensive as does "The Pangolin." "The Jerboa" concludes with the jerboa, whose grace is his own; "The Pangolin," with forty-four lines, almost half the poem, on the only creature for whom grace is ambiguous, an achievement or a gift.

The difference is that between the unfallen and the fallen creature, between a straightforward attraction that may invite sentimental responses (it is easy to love a jerboa) and the more complex and ambivalent attitudes that must be confronted if one is to love people, stuffy, ridiculous, pathetic, and fine as they characteristically are. Is it easy to love an eight-armed cephalopod, the subject of "The Paper Nautilus"? From one point of view, the poem represents a retreat from "The Pangolin," a falling back on the easier attractiveness of the pre-moral world and its creatures. The nautilus's egg-case is lovely, unmarred by such irony-evoking, man-made grotesqueries as "Like does not like like that is obnoxious" or "error" spelled with four r's; and we know, if we were ever in any doubt, that she does not construct her thin glass shell for people, those serge-clad, strong-shod mammals who for the moment seemed to have the last word in "The Pangolin." Only the nautilus knows that "love/ is the only fortress/ strong enough to trust to," and single-mindedly acts accordingly, with results of surprising strength and delicacy.

But this reading may be, and I suspect is, misleading. The nautilus's capacity for love is, after all, an "as if," a figurative thing. The figurativeness of it all is even more delicately emphasized in the assertion that it is not the nautilus but the nautilus's arms that act "as if they knew love/ is the only fortress/ strong enough to trust to," and it could have been "as if she knew" if Miss Moore had wanted it that way, the nautilus having been "she" twice already in the poem. In a small, but precise and persistent, way we are being warned not to be deceived, not to see the nautilus as an exemplar of that "aspect of humanity which is prefigured, and no more than that," [23] in the defense of an egg-case. The poem may be not a denial but a recapitulation of "The Pangolin," its movement not from unsatisfactory man to admirable shellfish but from the diagrammatic to the ineffable.

And if "The Paper Nautilus" says explicitly less about its human object than does "The Pangolin," that may be because the shorter poem has to do with what C. S. Lewis, writing about Spenser (and, like Miss Moore in "The Pangolin," about grace), has called "the virtue behind the virtue," lacking which, "we shall still be clumsy, unless the Graces come and dance with us, unless a beauty which no man can achieve by effort flows into our daily acts of its own will." [24] Lewis' preoccupations are not excessively theological for application to Miss Moore. In a 1958 article of counsel for the young, "If I Were Sixteen Today," Miss Moore concludes:

One should above all, learn to be silent, to listen; to make possible promptings from on high. Suppose you "don't believe in God." Talk to someone very wise, who believed in God, did not, and then found that he did. The cure for loneliness is solitude. [One may recall the cardinal's remarks in "Smooth Gnarled Crape Myrtle."] Think about this saying by Martin Buber: "The free man believes in destiny and that it has need of him." Destiny, not fate.

And lastly, ponder Solomon's wish: when God appeared to him in a dream and asked, "What wouldst thou that I give unto thee?" Solomon did not say fame, power, riches, but an understanding heart, and the rest was added. [25]

And for whatever the fact may be worth as a suggestion of associations, Miss Moore begins the article by quoting herself, the phrase "hindered to succeed," from "The Paper Nautilus": "When I was sixteen—in fact thirteen—I felt as old as at any time since; and what I wish I could have been when sixteen I am trying to be now—'hindered to succeed.' " [26] The ultimate form of such hindrance is one's mortality, and the ultimate success that may spring from it is the transformation of mortality into eternity that courage and love at one level, grace at another, make possible.

What Are Years? moves triumphantly from courage to love; *Nevertheless* opens in much the same way, with instances of hindered mortality rising upon itself to demonstrate that even in the vegetable world there is nothing like fortitude. But it is a different book—more troubled, more aware or more painfully aware of the distance between commitment to belief or principle and the uncomfortable facts of immediate emotional experience. It moves from simple praise of fortitude, in the title poem, to something much more complicated and uncertain in the last, "In Distrust of Merits," a poem that, echoing many earlier poems, shifts uncertainly between an effort to assume a burden of responsibility for the Second World War and a sin-ridden sense of the task's impossibility. It is Auden's "We must love one another or die," [27] but without Auden's perhaps unconvincing cheeriness in his poem's concluding lines, and equally without Auden's framework of historical determinism and his clear sense of purpose. The fight to be affectionate is still the central fact of moral experience, the one overriding categorical imperative that Miss Moore recognizes, but here it is supported by no ironic or triumphant rhetoric. This poem, more starkly than Auden's, expresses the abiding fear that the fight may be a lost cause.

Does it sum up its volume? Perhaps not. At least the certainties of "Nevertheless" ("The weak overcomes its/ menace, the strong over-/ comes itself") have become uncertain, and the other four poems in the book do little to prepare us for the expense of spirit that "In Distrust of Merits" involves. "The Wood-Weasel" is a delightful bit of album verse, constructed as an upside-down acrostic; its skunk, beautiful, independent, and in charge of things, is also playful, but clearly on his own terms and with his own kind. He will never blame himself for inwardly doing nothing, never feel the need to recover from the disease, My Self. He is, in fact, one of the weak, who overcome their menace; but his merits, real as they are, are among those distrusted in the final poem, symptoms of illness rather than evidences of health, at least when they appear in people.

Both strength and weakness manifest themselves in "Elephants," with its "defenseless human thing" asleep on a sleeping elephant, "invincibly tusked, made safe by magic hairs!" And "Elephants" too seems to offer a point of view at odds with that of "In Distrust of Merits." The elephants, Socratic beasts who have overcome themselves by accepting the fact of loss and gravely cooperating with their human captors, preserve dignity and integrity and in general exemplify the uses of adversity so well that they seem an embodiment of the best in man, a kind of gently ponderous Houyhnhnm who really knows the brotherhood of creatures and in that knowledge permits himself to be used. Perhaps one has to say that it is this view of possibilities that has collapsed in "In Distrust of Merits," or that needs reasserting in a harder context. Or perhaps it is necessary to pay more attention than one tends to in a first reading to the sixth stanza's brief and surprising outburst, "As if, as if, it is all ifs; we are at/ much unease." The poem pulls away quickly from this particular direction, but it may be the critical moment in the poem, the brief and compact warning that we are not simply being invited to play "Let's pretend." Elephants seem to teach us philosophic resignation, like that of the condemned Socrates.

But Socrates comes back into the poem in the closing lines— the skeptical Socrates, for whom even philosophical resignation may not be a final answer, as of course it is not in "In Distrust of Merits." Even in the *Apology*, the meaning of death is an iffy thing for Socrates; in fact, it is possible to wonder whether

Socrates was not rather a rider on tigers than a sleeper on elephants. One knows what Miss Moore means, or at least one supposes one does; granted that it is all ifs, life is more stable, less tendentious and liable to self-destruction, if one lives as if one had an elephant rather than a tiger under one. But "In Distrust of Merits" is the final poem in *Nevertheless,* and deliberately so; in terms of original publication, only "The Wood-Weasel" is earlier; "In Distrust of Merits" comes last because Miss Moore wanted it to come last. And what it does to the other poems is to throw their innocences into sharp relief. Like *What Are Years?, Nevertheless* is a book in praise of courage and love, but its dynamic is less the sense of grace than it is the loss of innocence. To sleep on an elephant may very well be repose, but it is the human condition to have to ride on tigers.

Innocence of a sort is also visible in "A Carriage from Sweden," and perhaps some degree of wistful evasion of the world in which tigers must be ridden. Hidden away somewhere in Brooklyn, "this city of freckled/ integrity," the carriage makes Miss Moore "feel at home." That feeling is presumably one of the "ifs" of "Elephants," a nostalgia for a simpler, sweeter world of unannoying romance in which stalwartness and skill are sufficient guarantees of integrity in both people and the things they make: "Carts are my trade." But against this stands "I inwardly did nothing" from "In Distrust of Merits." Private integrity may be personal self-indulgence; to feel at home may be, for a creature whose nature it is to ride on tigers, a dangerous luxury. "Beauty is everlasting," says "In Distrust of Merits"; and if mortal aspiration is eternity, as in "What Are Years?," still "dust is for a time" and behaves at its peril—its moral peril—when it attempts to find rest in some timeless absolute.

"The Mind Is an Enchanting 'Thing" is apparently a war poem. In a note prepared for the Kimon Friar-John Malcolm Brinnin anthology *Modern Poetry*, Miss Moore wrote: "One of the winters between 1930 and 1940, Gieseking gave at the Brooklyn Academy, a program of Handel, Bach, and Scarlatti, the moral of this poem being that there is something more important than outward rightness. One doesn't get through with the fact that Herod beheaded John the Baptist, 'for his oath's sake'; as one doesn't, I feel, get through with the injustice of the deaths died in the war, and in the first world war." [28] But it is difficult to state the relationship between these particular moral insights and the poem as text, or between "The Mind Is an Enchanting Thing" and "In Distrust of Merits." I suspect that the connection has something to do with the ambiguities of enchantment, which may be a very good thing, the opposite of disenchantment, or which may be a very bad thing, subjection to illusion or to uncanny power. The "fire in the dove-neck's/ iridescence" is lovely, but it is not really there, or at least is not really fire; and the ability to "hear without/ having to hear" may induce hearing what was never said. Fortunately, the mind does not insist on an either-or sort of awareness, preferring to be "conscientiously inconsistent"; if it gives us a world of the odd and the lovely, it also

> tears off the veil; tears
> the temptation, the
> mist the heart wears,
> from its eyes—if the heart
> has a face. . . .

Left to itself, the heart presumably prefers outward rightness and Herod's oath, the unchanging absolute, beauty that is everlasting, Sweden, stalwartness, and skill. It sees what it wants to see—happy skunks, philosophic elephants, courageous prickly-pear leaves. But even such heartfelt unconfusion has its confusions for the mind to deal with, and "In Distrust of Merits" gives them its full attention.

"In Distrust of Merits" owes much of its special quality in the Moore canon to its conspicuous refusal to simplify the heart's confusions. This of course is not new with Miss Moore; she has always been attracted by dialectically related impulses to generalize and to particularize,[29] but it may be safe to say that as a rule such tensions resolve themselves in some witty synthesis—the image of a steam roller, a statue of Daniel Webster, an imaginary garden with real toads in it. Even "Virginia Britannia" has its great closing image of particularities gradually absorbed into sunset, cloudscape, and gathering darkness as an intimation of glory. "In Distrust of Merits" offers no such synthesizing image, only its final sense of helpless, almost hopeless guilt and inadequacy, like that of Milton's Samson before his testing. Its closing aphorism—"Beauty is everlasting/ and dust is for a time"—is less a synthesis than it is a giving up, a taking refuge in the fact that life is finite. As we have seen,[30] Miss Moore has expressed herself as dissatisfied with the poem on formal grounds, and in a way it is perfectly clear that she is right.

I suppose the real trouble is that "In Distrust of Merits" deals with intolerables. "It's truthful," Miss Moore says; "it is testimony—to the fact that war is intolerable, and unjust."[31] And here, as perhaps always in such cases, the statement serves to suppress partially the more disturbing subject of the moral status and responsibility of those, particularly oneself, who tolerate the intolerable, who inwardly do nothing. The poem's final judgment is clear: these are the ultimate betrayers; the Iscariot-like crime is one's own, as it has been since the third stanza:

> they're fighting that I
> may yet recover from the disease, My
> Self.

Recovery is at best partial, perhaps not even that; in stanza five, "we are not competent to make our vows," not even, presumably, the one we have just made, never to hate. Others' sacrifices cure me; "or am I what I can't believe in?"—that is, incurable. "'When a man is prey to anger,/ he is moved by outside things'"; but the speaker here is much moved by outside things. And to hold one's ground "'in patience patience/ patience' . . . the soldier's defense/ and hardest armor for/ the fight," differs from inwardly doing nothing chiefly in terms of one's own feeling about it and oneself. Such feeling here does not modulate; it swoops, between detachment and revulsion from detachment. A. Kingsley Weatherhead remarks finely of the manner here:

Is not this new style rather a symbolic act of dispossession and self-deprivation insofar as it is a sacrifice of the advantages of the other style, which is an integral part of the poet's personality? The sentiment that

> . . . I must
> fight till I have conquered in myself what
> causes war . . .

calls for a sweeping distrust and questioning of *all* one's merits, including one's skill at controlling feeling. Perhaps in the face of the great catastrophe, the exercise of her habitual artistic strategy looked to her like a precious interest in personal cleverness.[32]

This is an attractive hypothesis, suggestive in its way of Yeats's turning against and remaking of himself early in the century. And as a matter of fact, "In Distrust of Merits" seems oddly full of a consciousness of past poems. Weatherhead remarks on resemblance between passages in "A Grave" and this poem:

> looking as if it were not that ocean in
> which dropped things are bound to sink—
> in which if they turn and twist, it is neither with
> volition nor consciousness,

and

> O tumultuous
> ocean, lashed till small things go
> as they will, the mountainous
> wave makes us who look, know
> depth. Lost at sea before they fought!

One can add, however, that the lashed world in which small things go as they will also echoes "The Fish," in which

> the stars,
> pink
> rice-grains, ink-
> bespattered jellyfish, crabs like green
> lilies, and submarine
> toadstools, slide each on the other.

The wave that makes us know depth suggests, however remotely, the abandoned "Melancthon":

Will
depth be depth, thick skin be thick, to one who can see no
beautiful element of unreason under it?

"The blessed deeds bless/ the halo," in stanza two, suggests the
frigate pelican's motto, "If I do well I am blessed/ whether any
bless me or not." The promise never to hate "black, white, red,
yellow, Jew,/ Gentile, Untouchable" is reminiscent of the
knowledge in "The Labors of Hercules" that

> the Negro is not brutal,
> that the Jew is not greedy,
> that the Oriental is not immoral,
> that the German is not a Hun.

In "He 'Digesteth Harde Yron,'" even brute courage knows
that "the power of the visible/ is the invisible"; "In Distrust of
Merits" speaks of the action or beauty that results from holding one's ground in patience, unmoved by outside things, and
both may recall the long-abandoned "Reinforcements":

> The pulse of intention does not move so that one
>   can see it, and moral machinery is not labelled, but
> the future of time is determined by the power of volition.

It would probably be excessive to suggest that "In Distrust of
Merits" involves a repudiation of these earlier formulations,
but it would not be excessive to point out that, in the later
poem, formulations do not hold with anything like the as-
surance of the earlier ones. And it may not be too much to
suggest that "In Distrust of Merits" represents a major attempt
to move beyond her habitual self-imposed limits of subject
matter and decorum. ("Miss Moore has great limitations—her
work is one long triumph of them." [33]) Perhaps it does not

work; certainly it is not complete and satisfying in the sense that "Peter" and "Critics and Connoisseurs" and "Bird-Witted" are; but knowledge of the intolerable rarely is.

"In Distrust of Merits" is a remarkable performance, but in its uninsistent way, a quite different way, the group of nine poems closing *Collected Poems* is equally remarkable, effecting something much like a musical modulation of key and final resolution. *Nevertheless* closes with an almost schizoid sense of personal fragmentation, of formulations that do not work, of duties to be carried out but that cannot be carried out, and of self-loathing. The mind's enchantment, in the destructive sense of the term, is virtually complete; it has looked into itself and found an abyss. "A Face," the first poem in the following section,[34] could be described as convalescent. Exasperated desperation, looking at itself in a mirror, finds no adequate basis for hating itself and realizes that, face to face with actuality, love of others remains a fact. It is a small but existentially significant moment of insight; like John Stuart Mill's discovery that he could weep, it makes life possible.

"By Disposition of Angels" perhaps carries the process of convalescence a bit further, dealing with the recovery of, and wonder over, the ability to respond to integrity and steadiness, "these unparticularities praise cannot violate."

> One has seen, in such steadiness never deflected,
> how by darkness a star is perfected.

This poem was first printed in 1948; seven years later, in a review of Louise Bogan's *Selected Criticism,* Miss Moore wrote: "She affirms Rilke's conviction that 'we must adhere to difficulty if we would make any claim to having a part in life' and feels that we have in Rilke 'one of the strongest antidotes to the powers of darkness'; 'often exhausted, often afraid, often in flight but capable of growth and solitude—he stands as an example of integrity held through and beyond change.' " [35] And something complicated seems to be going on here. One cannot well be influenced in 1948 or earlier by something one has read in 1955, but the two Bogan essays on Rilke from which Miss Moore quotes first appeared in 1937 and 1940,[36] well prior to "By Disposition of Angels." And that poem has in fact an oddly Rilke-esque look to it. The angels of Rilke's *Duino Elegies*, to be sure, are not "messengers much like ourselves," but Miss Moore is not sure that hers are either; like Rilke's, they are "above particularities," to be defined only by questions or by those "mysteries [that] expound mysteries." Rilke speaks of his angel as "the creature in whom that transformation of the visible into the invisible [we may remember "the power of the visible/ is the invisible"] we are performing already appears completed. . . . The Angel of the Elegies is the being who vouches for the recognition of a higher degree of reality in the invisible." [37]

"By Disposition of Angels" concerns itself with such a recognition. Miss Moore's list of rhetorical questions about angels may be reminiscent of Rilke's similar rhetorical questioning of the Angel in the Second Elegy:

> Who are you?
> Early successes, favourites of fond Creation,
> ranges, summits, dawn-red ridges
> of all beginning,—pollen of blossoming godhead,
> hinges of light, corridors, stairways, thrones,
> spaces of being, shields of felicity, tumults

> of stormily-rapturous feeling, and suddenly, separate,
> mirrors, drawing up their own
> outstreamed beauty into their faces again.[38]

The Angel as a self-contained mirror may or may not suggest the mirror gesture of "A Face," but the angels' ideal steadiness in Miss Moore's poem is very like their self-sufficiency in Rilke's, measured against human evanescence: "For we, when we feel, evaporate." [39] And Miss Moore's "Star that does not ask me if I see it?" has a great deal in common both with the Rilkean angel's indifference to the human and, by antithesis, with the First Elegy's

> Yes, the Springs had need of you. Many a star
> was waiting for you to espy it.[40]

Wallace Fowlie remarks that Miss Moore "owes nothing, specifically, to other poets," [41] but this poem suggests otherwise. As an "example of integrity held through and beyond change," [42] Rilke may have been of much value to the poet of "In Distrust of Merits," and perhaps of even more value in view of the death, in the preceding year, of Mary Warner Moore, the poet's mother, who for years had functioned as resident critic and apparently as her daughter's closest personal friend. Mrs. Moore had approved of "A Face" after declaring "It won't do" of something else; and since "A Face" was written in response to a request from Cyril Connolly "for something for *Horizon*," appearing there in October, 1947, it may well have been one of the last poems on which Mrs. Moore's judgment could have been sought.[43] "By Disposition of Angels" may also be a tribute to Mrs. Moore.[44]

"The Icosasphere" moves from "unparticularities praise cannot violate" to particularities: the hedge-sparrow's nest, perfect of its instinctive sort; a squalid human scramble after an unearned fortune, another revelation of the abyss; and the minor but solid human achievement of steel spheres and vertical granite monoliths. This has something in common with "A Carriage from Sweden" in its praise of craftsmanship and making but without the earlier poem's concentrated idyllicism; Mrs. Garrett's fortune leaves no room for that. And "His Shield" indicates that even such grubby manifestations of the human need not appall one properly armored with freedom, "the power of relinquishing/ what one would keep." We are back to "The Hero," the man who "covets nothing that [he] has let go"; some sort of recovery seems to have been completed.

But even this formulation is shaky. " 'Keeping Their World Large' " does not altogether recapitulate the crisis of "In Distrust of Merits," but like the earlier poem it too finds no way to make affirmations out of the war. That the war dead have relinquished the life they would presumably have preferred to keep is indisputable; their shield, one may say, was their humility, and it did not save them. Our shield, on the other hand, is their flesh and their spirit, and in its way it did save us, though "the very heart was a prayer/ against this way of victory." [45] This singularly brutal irony, whereby men die in order to make the world safe for "fat living and self-pity," makes a mockery of personal righteousness, of "merits." It is one thing to be willing to relinquish what one would keep; it is quite another to survive comfortably because of another's proven willingness to do the same thing. Personal righteousness, private morality, saves nothing when it is merely personal and private, and hence " 'Keeping Their World Large' " is followed by "Efforts of Affection," an echo of the movement from major denial in "In Distrust of Merits" to small affirmation in "A Face."

"Efforts of Affection" differs from "A Face" chiefly, I suppose, in being less a product of crisis—more whimsical, more playful, more deliberately elliptical. It drifts into its moderate praise of love as if by purely random associations from the occupational specialties of Cain's descendants to Bottom's odd taste in light refreshment, and perhaps Titania's taste for Bottom, to La Fontaine's devotion—to the fables? to Madame de Sévigné?—to love as a means of assuring integrity—"integration," a term carried over from "The Icosasphere" for the quality so conspicuously lacking in Mrs. Garrett's would-be heirs. Love won't do everything: "You know I'm not a saint!" But sanctity is not necessary ("that strange rubber fern's attraction/ puts perfume to shame") and clearly must not be expected ("Unsheared sprays of elephant-ears/ Do not make a selfish end look like a noble one"). Even love can corrupt as well as rectify; like the sun, it "can rot or mend," as the sun at the end of " 'Keeping Their World Large' " shines ambiguously on the sick scene. But the love that unites, that mends, that generates wholeness—a dangerous abstraction, that; better, simply, the healthy sort, and that begs the question—at least, the love that tries to direct itself toward others may be a value that endures. We have recovered the fight to be affectionate.

And this means that even mild personal preference has its place, as in "Voracities and Verities Sometimes Are Interacting." Here, fondness for emeralds rather than diamonds, for the unobtrusive varieties of gratitude, for poetry such as

elephants write, and for a book about tigers someone unidentified knows of ("I think you know the one." This poem
too was first printed in 1947, the year of Mary Warner Moore's
death; the appearance of coyness may be rather a clear sense
of audience.) are testimonies to love and grounds for forgive-
ness. Regarding tigers, one may or may not recall, from "Efforts
of Affection," that "love can make one/ bestial or make a beast
a man"; regarding unexcessive gratitude, from "'Keeping Their
World Large,'" "Tears that don't fall are what/ they wanted";
regarding "unobtrusiveness [that] is dazzling," the useful advice from "His Shield," "be/ dull." Such almost pre-logical associations, echoing vaguely in one's mind as one reads, provide
the illusion at least of continuous and ultimately unitary experience. I am not sure but that the disarmingly titled *Collected Later* (1951) may be Miss Moore's most tightly constructed volume, "a tuned reticence with rigor/ from strength
at the source," as "Propriety" puts it. In this poem, mere statement of preference passes into a half-whimsical attempt to
understand it; predictably, that propriety shared by Bach and
Brahms, or Brahms and Bach, lies in both men's being "un-
cursed by self-inspection"—and one may recall from "Efforts
of Affection" the "unself-righteousness" that "humbles inspection." As was true of the child with the pup in "Critics and
Connoisseurs," so with Bach and Brahms: right behavior, behavior to which one responds with gratitude and approval, is
largely a matter of unconscious fastidiousness, of fastidiousness
I suppose so deeply practiced as to be as unintentional as a
pansy's face, the self armored against undue exposure by its
own habitual competence for the task at hand.

But this is still too easy, too simple, too diagrammatic and hence vulnerable. "Armor's Undermining Modesty" brings things finally back into the tragic focus of "What Are Years?," "Virginia Britannia," and "The Pangolin." "There is the tarnish; and there, the imperishable wish," in the same place. All are still naked, none are yet safe, and the tarnish and the wish, like Eliot's fire and rose, or like the love that can either rot or mend, are one. Moths may be simply and unambiguously lovely; but ambiguity has been an inescapable condition of the human ever since man first discovered he was a self and asserted the discovery in stone axes and alphabets, making possible technology, war, puns, etymology, and symbols, those ambiguous determinants of life's faulty excellence. Without them, we cannot be implicit; with them, we can be pretentious, or worse. Without them, we have no Grails to seek; with them, we have "wreaths and silver rods, and armor gilded/ or inlaid," trappings of the quest that may eventually replace the quest. Without them, there is no way to give meaning and precision to life; with them, there are too many ways to let self bar one's usefulness to others who are different.

This extraordinarily elliptical poem becomes even more elliptical in its concluding stanzas (Randall Jarrell, once more, observes, "I don't entirely understand it, but what I understand I love, and what I don't understand I love almost better." [46]), though some degree of difficulty is simplified if we assume a misprint in stanza six. In both *Collected Poems* and *Complete Poems,* the first word of line four is "is"; in the poem's first printing in *The Nation* for February 25, 1950, the word is "in," to the considerable clarification of syntax at least. Even so, the remark about Mars and heroes seems dark, and attempts at paraphrase particularly clumsy. The point, I suspect, is that heroes' conduct makes clear enough what they hate; they need not spell it out, even though war's excess (in violence? in heroism? in the negatives of mere prevention rather than in the positives of usefulness to others?) makes it hard to see clearly—ambiguity, again. Excess, at any rate, is one of those things they hate. I am not clear whether the heroes here are the old Grail-seeking *ducs,* in which case they presumably have literal armor, though not gilded or inlaid; or whether they are twentieth-century soldiers, as in "In Distrust of Merits" and " 'Keeping Their World Large,' " in which case they do not. It makes a difference, if only in the sense that a discussion of armor's ambiguous advantages and disadvantages, its capacity for undermining one's modesty or its modesty that undermines others, will have different overtones depending on whether one's conversational opposite is wearing it or not. What is clear is that ambiguity is piling up; armor may be a threat to one's virtue, or it may be a virtue itself; it may be a symptom of, or a remedy for, excess; it may be a form of, or it may undermine, innocent depravity. It may be a form of continence (continence: the state of being contained, as by a suit of armor), or it may not ("A mirror-of-steel uninsistence should" —but often does not—"countenance continence"). It may be a means toward a Miltonic paradise within, "of innocence and altitude/ in an unhackneyed solitude"; or it may be a source of those terrible illusions of innocence that, more precise than precision, motivate the "blind man who/ can see," of "In Distrust of Merits." "There is the tarnish; and there, the imperishable wish," and the one is the cost of the other.

"Good and evil," declared Milton, "we know in the field of this World grow up almost inseparably; and the knowledge of good is so involv'd and interwoven with the knowledge of evill, and in so many cunning resemblances hardly to be discern'd, that those confused seeds which were impos'd on *Psyche* as an incessant labour to cull out, and sort asunder, were not more intermixt. It was from out the rinde of one apple tasted, that the knowledge of good and evill as two twins cleaving together leapt forth into the World. And perhaps this is that doom which *Adam* fell into of knowing good and evill, that is to say of knowing good by evill." [47] Miss Moore is not Milton, but she shares his tradition in some important ways. Milton's Protestant humanism, with its emphasis on man as fallen but heroic, as responsible for his own desperations but capable of surviving them, and as dependent for guidance largely on *recta ratio* and his own experience—Milton's humanism differs from Miss Moore's with respect to magnitude and to philosophical and theological explicitness. But Pope's humanism differs from Milton's in much the same way, and if these poems of the 1930s and 1940s cannot be thought of as "Paradise Lost" or "Samson Agonistes," they are a more than respectable "Essay on Man."

CHAPTER 6

The Mogul's Dream

Collected Poems appeared in 1951; since then, in addition to receiving the honors paid her for that volume,[1] Marianne Moore has published two volumes of translation, one of adaptation, one of her own critical and appreciative writings, and three of original verse, as well as *A Marianne Moore Reader* and *Complete Poems*. The three books of poems, largely unchanged, constitute most of Part II of *Complete Poems*. And on the whole it seems safe to say that they do little to alter the sense of her accomplishment that *Collected Poems* makes evident. There is no particular reason why they should; *Collected Poems* needs no postscript to justify its existence. But in a culture that traditionally values achievement, Miss Moore at eighty-one raises the problem of evaluating the late work of a poet whose principal achievement is probably complete.

Miss Moore herself, always deprecatory about her own writing, seems especially so about her late work. Though she sees no reason for not continuing to write,[2] she does not, and perhaps never has, taken that continuation for granted. In 1961 she told Donald Hall, apropos of never having intended to write poetry, "And now, too, I think each time I write that it may be the last time; then I'm charmed by something and seem to have to say something."³ And again: "If I get a promising idea I set it down, and it stays there. I don't make myself do anything with it. I've had several things in the *New Yorker*. And I said to them, 'I might never write again,' and not to expect me to." ⁴ She writes, in fact, to satisfy herself, as to be sure she always did ("It is for himself that the writer writes, charmed or exasperated to participate; eluded, arrested, enticed by felicities." ⁵). But the poems of these late volumes in a way seem to matter less to her. The volumes themselves seem less constructions, like *Collected Poems* and its component parts, than collections; *Like a Bulwark,* in which Miss Moore lists dates of publication as part of her acknowledgments, appears to be a straight chronological assembly of poems, without the concern for arrangement evident in *What Are Years?* and *Collected Later*. And though, as Randall Jarrell observes, "it is most barbarously unjust to treat her . . . as what she is only when she parodies herself," ⁶ nevertheless the tendency to self-parody, if that is what it is, manifests itself in these late poems. "In This Age of Hard Trying, Nonchalance Is Good and" has a sharply defined point, even though one may be quite unclear what that point is; "A Jellyfish," on the other hand, seems perfectly clear, but has very little to be clear about. "To a Snail" was short and brilliant; "O to Be a Dragon" is only short.

There is, of course, another way to regard these contrasts. "In This Age of Hard Trying, Nonchalance Is Good and" may be suspected of pretending to say much more than it really does, of being all machinery and no function, like a Rube Goldberg creation; "A Jellyfish" makes no pretense to delivering more than its own precise but limited observation. "O to Be a Dragon" can enter the same modest claim, exemplifying principles laid down in "To a Snail":

> It is not the acquisition of any one thing
> that is able to adorn,
> or the incidental quality that occurs
> as a concomitant of something well said,
> that we value in style,
> but the principle that is hid.

Here, the hid principle has something to do with the poem's dizzying, and perhaps self-mocking, shifts in tone from that of the play-acting wisdom seeker ("If I, like Solomon . . . / could have my wish—/ my wish . . .") to that of the wistful gusher ("O to be a dragon,/ a symbol of the power of Heaven— of silkworm/ size or immense; at times invisible.") to that of the pedantically pleased and slightly dippy school mistress summing up everything and nothing ("Felicitous phenomenon!"). In its own way, it is an extraordinarily funny poem, and it sums up certain preoccupations of Miss Moore's,[7] though one must approach it with almost infinite tolerance in order to enjoy it.

That may be the problem with these later poems: they demand tolerance. "Like a Bulwark" (first printed in *Botteghe Oscure*, then in the *Saturday Review of Literature*, as "At Rest in the Blast"; revised and collected in the volume *Like a Bulwark* as "Bulwarked Against Fate"; reprinted in *A Marianne Moore Reader* and *Complete Poems* as "Like a Bulwark") seems a case in point. It says that resistance strengthens one and that the strong endure. There would be no point in quarreling with the statement or with Miss Moore's admiration for the person, real or hypothetical, who exemplifies it. Yet the poem is essentially rhetoric, with little indeed of the fine surprise that makes "Nevertheless," for example, something more than its rhetoric. It remains a verbalized thought for the day, admirable in its way, applicable in its way. But it moves one less to admiration than to sympathy, like the grotesque episode with the Ford Motor Company in 1955 as that corporation labored to find a new name for a new car—a name that would "have a compelling quality in itself and by itself. To convey, through association or other conjuration, some visceral feeling of elegance, fleetness, and advanced features and design. A name, in short, that flashes a dramatically desirable picture in people's minds." [8] "Like a Bulwark" is not really this kind of rubbish, if only because it is concerned with a moral posture rather than the Edsel. But both the letter and the poem grope for instead of presenting; both are a variety of thinking out loud, a kind of verbal doodling; and both, I suspect, owe what interest they may have to the fact that Marianne Moore was involved with them.

There is something to be said for getting one's harshest comment out of the way in one bilious lump, and I propose to do that now. Some of Miss Moore's feeblest work is in these late volumes, work about which there is simply nothing to be said except that she wrote it and has found it worthy of being preserved, which may, of course, be all that needs saying. Be that as it may, here are private games ("To Victor Hugo of My Crow Pluto"), private passions ("Hometown Piece for Messrs. Alston and Reese"), and private causes ("The Camperdown Elm"); unfunny jokes ("Dream"), doggerel couplets ("Values in Use," "Hometown Piece . . . ," "Enough," "I've Been Thinking," "To Victor Hugo . . ."), and tortuously oblique associations that one breaks one's back over and that may have become largely habitual ("Tell Me, Tell Me," perhaps, or "Then the Ermine," or "Logic and 'The Magic Flute' "). It may be significant that in *Selected Poems* and *Collected Poems,* her characteristic gesture toward earlier work was to reject it;[9] here, it is to readmit. "Like a Bulwark," first printed in 1948, was available for *Collected Poems* but not included there; "I May, I Might, I Must," "To a Chameleon," and "Sun" are retitled versions of old poems, whose reappearance may suggest some relaxing of standards of self-criticism. And it is hard to imagine "The Camperdown Elm" appearing in *What Are Years?*

I suspect that there are two elements involved in these rumblings of critical gastritis, neither of which is quite an appropriate object of literary criticism. One is simply the matter of age; few people live, at seventy or eighty, in the way they did at forty or fifty, and there seems little reason to suppose that they either will or should write in the same way. Here as elsewhere there is much to be said for the notion that, from about sixty-five on, one has earned the right to live as one wishes, or can, to write for oneself and the Camperdown elm. In doing so, one may become a crank, a hobby-rider, an entertainer of oneself. David Daiches remarks of Yeats, in his last poems: "We are a little scared of this rapt old man shouting strange cold words at us," [10] and if Marianne Moore hardly frightens, she may disappoint. And that is the second of my two grounds for critical unhappiness, an element of something very like mere personal disappointment—that the resonant voice of "In Distrust of Merits" and "Virginia Britannia" and

"Armor's Undermining Modesty" fades out, that the apparently organized sequences of the earlier work tend to become random or mechanical sequences; that, in fact, Miss Moore at eighty is not Miss Moore at sixty.

Within the limits imposed by such constitutional biases, what is there to be said for these late poems? Quite a bit, as a matter of fact. In *Like a Bulwark*, "Apparition of Splendor" provides in its porcupine a microcosmic equivalent of the forest it inhabits and a half-whimsical embodiment of that unbellicose resistance to fate celebrated in the title poem, which directly precedes it. Dürer's rhinoceros, a remarkable creature wearing what appears to be an elaborate suit of link, scale, and plate armor,[11] provides a less splendid, because never known literally, apparition; it also suggests that "Then the Ermine," the next poem in the book, is to be associated by virtue of its closing reference to "violets by Dürer." But the association is not particularly helpful; the poem puzzles, chiefly, it seems to me, from a basic uncertainty of intent, whether it is in praise of integrity or of flexibility. It juxtaposes mottoes involving singleness and wholeness against the odd uncertainties of actual experience. But the point about Lavater's physiography remains elusive; perhaps it represents a successful attempt to remain unspotted and unchanged despite the flux of experience. The puzzling "it" in the first line of stanza six is the result of revision for *Complete Poems* of a much clearer passage in the *Like a Bulwark* version: "So let the *palisandre* settee express/ change," which seems to favor life and flexibility rather than the rigidities imposed by hammer-handed bravado—crows and shepherdesses together rather than a Herod's oath that cannot change. But "foiled explosiveness" is another puzzle. Challenged ingenuity can produce something, but conviction is hard to arrive at. Thus mixing unlikes, crows and shepherdesses, might be expected to lead to trouble, did not the palisandre settee, like Wallace Stevens' blue guitar, change them, making them perfect like Dürer's violets and thus concealing their original instability and turning it inward, giving them the power of implosion, inward energy ("The power of the visible/ is the invisible," as the ostrich knows in "He 'Digesteth Harde Yron.'"). Art changes everything, from violets to rhinoceroses, but this poem remains a complicated puzzle.

"Tom Fool at Jamaica" suggests that to be an enthusiast is one thing, to be the victim of an infallible system, quite another. Jonah was almost such a victim but recovered in time, and other victims go with the race track setting, especially those implicit in Signor Capossela's explanation of his success in announcing races: "I'm relaxed, I'm confident, and I *don't bet*." No hammer-handed bravado here, though there might be the makings of a Herod's oath. Enthusiasm of the right sort is visible in the mule and jockey who were willing to stop when circumstances demanded; in Signor Capossela, who keeps his head; in Fats Waller, with the feather touch; and in others who, magnetized by feeling, do not thereby lose control. But Tom Fool, the horse, beats them all, and I want to be stuffy here for a moment. Up to about the time of *What Are Years?*, with "The Pangolin" as critical poem, Miss Moore's animal poems, though looking toward people, clearly preferred the simpler creatures who prefigured them—jerboas, basilisks, frigate pelicans. The hard job of preferring people, sticky and complicated as they are, was accomplished in the thirties and forties; and now in these later poems the animals seem to be coming back. Tom Fool has only to run; Signor Capossela has to discriminate; but the horse is the hero. Similarly, the very attractive "The Arctic Ox (or Goat)" looks no farther than its animal, unless by the most elliptical of routes; it is perhaps the least man-centered of her animal poems. Contrariwise, to be complete, "To a Giraffe," though another puzzle, seems to work in much the same way as did "To Statecraft Embalmed," its creature serving chiefly as mask for some human object. Here, as elsewhere, infallible systems hold only within fallible limits. And even in "Tom Fool at Jamaica" we may note that it is people who make judgments and respond to the magnificent horse, who see him as embodying the principle *sentir avec ardeur*.

The same principle justifies Italy in "The Web One Weaves of Italy." A multiplicity of things to see, it seems mere show compared with the intellectual life of the Sorbonne, but "Because the heart is in it all is well." *Sentir avec ardeur*, in fact, like the virologist in "The Staff of Aesculapius," "too impassioned to desist" from his research, or like the various exemplars of style in the poem of that name. In "The Sycamore," a monochromatic tree trunk serves as a reminder that "there's more than just one kind of grace" and suggests that those who prefer death to spottedness in "Then the Ermine" are missing a good bit; *ardeur* may as properly devote itself to assisting memory by painting a bug in the grass as to curing cancer or winning races. And in "Rosemary" the "herb of memory," its once-white flowers turned blue in imitation of Mary's robe during the flight into Egypt, evidently does not say *"mutare sperno"* nor reject such variously spotted roles as something that is simultaneously symbol and pungency may be called upon to carry. "Style" looks for a way of summing up what is common to two dancers, a guitar player, and a court tennis champion, and finds none: "There is no suitable simile." Certainly the simile of setting to music the structure of a banana seems more odd than suitable, and the face of Palestrina by El Greco does not really express the difference between different excellences, all of which embody style. The poem is finally reduced to simply enumerating its exemplars, pointing, as it were, to its separate spots.

"Logic and 'The Magic Flute'" calls for a good deal of guesswork, but like the palisandre settee in "Then the Ermine" it works by bringing together seeming incompatibles into a *Gestalt* that proves once more the interdependability of wholeness and miscellaneousness. Miss Moore's etymological note to line eleven enables us to suppose that a spiral shell near or on a television set (Winthrop Sargeant tells us that her apartment contains "a vast collection of miscellaneous objects she has amassed over the years." [12]) with a broadcast of "The Magic Flute" coming through suggests opera house stairs. The light on the screen might seem the ghost of a sunbeam or moonbeam, and neither sunbeams nor wentletraps have waists, though it is hard to see why the fact seemed worthy of note. Stanza two adds *Life* and *Time* to the *Gestalt*, together with the electronic hum of the television set and the darkness of the room, like the darkness inside a shell ("abalonean gloom"—does this have some quirky relationship with Yeats's "Babylonian starlight" in "Two Songs from a Play"?). Still more complexity, more spottedness, appears in an ice ballet scene, perhaps between acts on the television screen, with its roaring demon that

might be an ice rink's piped-in music or might be a monstrous
version of Mozart's Tamino, with overtones of the Moor
Monastatos, calling down the stairs provided by the wentletrap.
Ovid answers, as another footnote tells us, though it is not
clear whether "fetter-feigning uncouth/ fraud" refers to sloth
or to the demon, or for that matter the person watching the
broadcast. At any rate, the Ovidian aphorism, like others in
this volume, does not work, logical though it sounds; "Trapper
Love" "illogically wove/ what logic can't unweave"—the absurd plot of "The Magic Flute," the experienced *Gestalt* of this
whole associated tangle of spots that you need not even put
yourself out for; the last line returns to the spiral staircase of
an ideal second balcony that is all one's own.

Winthrop Sargeant, again, comments admirably on the
dynamics of this sort of poem:

Her capacity for stepping up the voltage of ordinary experience is
so great that the most commonplace happening or encounter becomes for her a major emotional event. . . . The primary source of
all this internal excitement is Miss Moore's wildly gymnastic self-
starting imagination, but once it swings into action it is liberally fed
by the combined resources of her singular gift for observing even
the smallest components of an object and her uncanny ability to remember everything she has observed. . . . Some of Miss Moore's
most rewarding adventures are trips to museums. "I get so excited
in them that before long I can't see anything," she says. To overcome this difficulty she has developed the habit of concentrating on
a single exhibit and firmly ignoring the rest; a few minutes spent in
this way give her all the stimulation she needs to make the expedi-
tion profitable, as the associations of what she has seen begin to
multiply in her mind by geometric progression.[13]

And as Miss Moore has said, of her own habit of quoting,

"When a thing has been said so well that it could not be said better, why paraphrase it?" [14]

"Blessed Is the Man" gives us, presumably, the satisfactory human embodiment of those virtues of endurance, integrity, steadiness, and conviction so ambiguously celebrated in other poems. Its sentiments are unexceptional, but it is, it seems to me, one of her least exciting performances. A catalog of unchallengeable virtues, it attacks with energy anonymous straw men—those who mongrelize anything they touch, geniuses who think egomania is a duty, men who do not take the risk of a decision, political lotus-eaters, brazen authors, and so on. Suggestively enough, it is one of the very few poems that Miss Moore has been defensive about.[15]

The later sections of *Collected Poems* seem to have been organized around and to express an emotional and intellectual crisis; *Like a Bulwark* is more loosely organized, "First this thought and then that," as she herself described "In Distrust of Merits";[16] but it has a kind of center in its persistent concern with tensions between wholeness and multiplicity, change and permanence, between that which can be rationalized into a formula and that which can only be experienced. *O to Be a Dragon* is still more loosely organized, though the evidence provided by dates of initial publication of its individual poems suggests something other than chronology as the organizing principle. (*Tell Me, Tell Me* changes the principle yet again by printing poems in reverse chronological order.) As we have seen,[17] it contains a number of old poems as well as new work. The title poem, evidently new, concerns those problems of identity that appear in *Like a Bulwark*. No more than the rosemary will its dragon say *"mutare sperno"*; its capacity to be anything or nothing and still to be a dragon expresses, though it does not resolve, a good many contradictions.

Chameleons too change yet remain chameleons, which may account for the reappearance of "To a Chameleon"; minimally, the same thing can be said of the jellyfish in "A Jellyfish." And "I May, I Might, I Must" deals with the necessary changes one must be prepared for if one is to confront such experiential difficulties as crossing fens. I suppose that chameleons, jellyfish, and fen-crossers all exemplify values in use, but the poem of that name seems extraordinarily oblique, a warning against undue abstraction in writing and speaking; someone is evidently being found guilty of violating his own standards. But the bit quoted in the poem, and equally the larger bit quoted in the note, is not hopelessly abstruse, even judged on its own ground; it is not clear that its means defeat its ends, as did those of the ibis in "To Statecraft Embalmed." Hugh Kenner's remark that "few of the later poems *enact* as did so many of the earlier ones their lesson of probity" [18] seems precisely applicable.

"Hometown Piece for Messrs. Alston and Reese" is about the Dodgers and a few other people; "Casey at the Bat" is still a better baseball poem. "Enough" says that the Jamestown settlers had a difficult time of it until they discovered that growing tobacco was economically sounder than looking for gold that wasn't there, and it concludes that their uncertain testing of liberty may find its fulfillment in our faith therein. Probably intended as warning, with its precautionary "if" in the last line, the poem comes dangerously close to sounding smug at the end; faith, as Robert Frost once said, is a most filling vapor. But "Melchior Vulpius," whose subject wrote an anthem in thanks for "conquering faith," does more with its filling. Faith is imaged forth in the analogy of music, an art which we have to trust because we cannot understand it; we experience its greatness, but we cannot say why it is great. It exists, men practice it, and it raises mere breath, as from an automaton, into contrapuntal magnificence. Resisting formula, motto, or rationalization, it reminds one of the conclusion of the abandoned "Melancthon":

> Will
> depth be depth, thick skin be thick to one who can see no
> beautiful element of unreason under it? [19]

"Convictions," Miss Moore writes, "are the result of experience," and "experience is almost certain to accept the fact that mystery is not just a nut which diligence can crack." [20] This remarkably shapely and compact little poem (we may note, for example, how the faith-death sequence in the rhyme words closing the first stanza gravely reverse themselves to death-faith after the second stanza's experience of music) indicates both that early convictions have remained valid for Miss Moore and that she has not lost her ability to do tightly controlled work. *"Mutare sperno,"* perhaps, applies to large things but not necessarily to small, as in "No Better Than a 'Withered Daffodil,'" in which an experienced change of mood, generated by the merest happenstance, creates values in the process of living, much in the manner of Robert Frost's "Dust of Snow."

"In the Public Garden" strikes me as the most impressive poem in *O to Be a Dragon,* accomplishing that note of warning that "Enough" doesn't bring off. Very delicately, what seems at first to be a mere random set of impressions finds its unemphatic focus in the situation of "those in the trans-shipment camp," whose circumstances modify, change, even give the lie to the sense of a purely delightful occasion. "Boston has a festival—/ compositely for all," but not for those in the transshipment camp. "They make some fine young men at Harvard," says the almost scriptural taxi-driver, but the young men from the trans-shipment camp do not go there. Someone gilds Faneuil Hall's grasshopper weather-vane, but not someone from the trans-shipment camp, whose occupants have no marketable skills. Spring produces its "more than usual/ bouquet of what is vernal," but in the trans-shipment camp the plants that matter are those that can be sold in the faint hope of achieving release. The visitor to King's Chapel can listen to the hymn,

> "My work be praise while
> others go and come. No more a stranger
> or a guest but like a child
> at home,"

but those in the trans-shipment camp have not that opportunity to be at home. Even "the Muses have a home and swans" in the Public Garden and its swan boats, but not those in the trans-shipment camp, for whom legend is not factual and freedom hangs by a thread. The point need not be labored, and it never strikes one as labored in the poem, where all works by implication. "The deepest feeling always shows itself in silence;/ not in silence, but restraint." [21] Restraint is also present in the unheard but rigorously maintained consonantal rhyming of lines one, two, and five in each stanza on the single "el" sound. This fine, troubled poem has kinship with "In Distrust of Merits" and " 'Keeping Their World Large.' " [22]

At the risk of detecting ingenuities that are not there, I

suggest that something complicated happens now. "In the Public Garden" is in its quiet way a poem of guilt and responsibility; "The Arctic Ox (or Goat)" celebrates a creature of uncomplicated innocence. The goat in question needs no pampering, loves to play, lives on willow leaves, provides clothing for people and nests for song birds, and, like Adam in Andrew Marvell's version of Paradise, may prefer to walk without a mate: he is like the reindeer of "Rigorists" without the complicating element of saving lives by being eaten. And he leads into the evasively formulated, or unformulated, wish for conversion, sanctity, or beatitude that concludes "Saint Nicholas." The movement is from an ambivalent content-discontent with the world as it is, the world of experience, to delight in the near-Blakeian image of innocence, to the "hardly, barely prayable prayer" (Eliot's phrase in "The Dry Salvages"; Miss Moore has praised Eliot for his "reticent candor and emphasis by understatement" [23]), half intensity and half moonshine, as in stanza three's whimsy about the moon bringing down marvelous things to wear. Efforts at paraphrase seem particularly clumsy here, largely because of the carefully casual way in which the wish for the beatific vision is approached and conditioned. At the start, Miss Moore is playing at being a child; by the end, she is playing at playing at being a child.

> Saint Nicholas, O Santa Claus,
>   would it not be the most
> prized gift that ever was!

Adults, not children, address the old gentleman as "Saint Nicholas"; "O Santa Claus" says that the child's capacity for desperately wanting what it wants has come up through the adult's playing; it also says something about the adult's self-mockery for playing such games; and a long, long way back it may, given the poem's subject, touch on the Gospel injunction, "Except ye be converted, and become as little children, ye shall not enter into the kingdom of heaven." [24]

Gifts and a saint also figure in "For February 14th," but at lower pressure; one suspects an unclarified puzzle in the first stanza, but whimsical wish-making clearly gets its comeuppance in the last stanza's witty turn to practical wisdom. And this may be related to the concluding aphorism of "Combat Cultural"; parts are not clearly cemented in "For February 14th," as they are in "Saint Nicholas," [25] or "In the Public Garden." "Combat Cultural" begins with images of "cementedness," singleness of purpose, then passes into a proliferating series of Russian dances, and finds its exemplum in a wrestling dance involving either two identically garbed dancers or one dancer ("just one person") in a sort of *trompe-l'oeil* performance wrestling with himself. In an equally *trompe-l'oeil* performance that echoes the conclusion of "Melchior Vulpius," Miss Moore, like the Duchess ("Everything's got a moral, if only you can find it."), tells us what the moral of that is. The voice once more is that of the dippy school mistress, though, as is true of Yeats's Crazy Jane and Tom the Lunatic, such voices need not imply frivolity.

"Leonardo da Vinci's" seems a case in point. The Nan-ai-ans' sack dance may not be an "objective symbolic of *sagesse*," but St. Jerome's production of the Vulgate Bible presumably is. Yet the poem, after its initial anecdote, seems a lunatic assembly of leonine associations demonstrating the proposition of "Armor's Undermining Modesty" that "Even gifted scholars lose their way/ through faulty etymology." Jerome looks like a lion, tapering waist and all; the Nile rises in Leo, thus making lion's-mouth fountains appropriate, both as fountains and as symbols of *sagesse,* since fountains are to water as Leo is to the Nile's rise as the Vulgate is to those in need of the Gospel; the Nile also rises in Abyssinia, which happens to be the country of Haile Selassie, the Conquering Lion of Judah and perhaps the descendant of Prester John, whose Nestorian Christianity goes back to the fifth century, as do the lion Jerome and his Vulgate. Kingsley Weatherhead notes that "the picture itself is leonine because its painter is Leonardo," [26] and Bernard Engel suggests, of the seemingly "sun-dyed" sketch, "that the sun shone especially during the zodiacal season of Leo and that in Christian mythology the lion, like the sun, traditionally has been emblematic of the resurrection of Christ." [27] Here, as in "Saint Nicholas," any wish remains hardly, barely prayable, to be approached with the utmost circuitousness and the least possible assertion of self; but "Blaze on, picture,/ saint, beast" is an assertion of the immortality of art—art that, in "In the Public Garden," though "admired in general,/ is always actually personal." And the personal component here, unspoken as in "Saint Nicholas," is the prayer for Christian immortality, a phenomenon more felicitous even than dragonhood.

Tell Me, Tell Me seems a thoroughly mixed grill, even omitting as it does in *Complete Poems* the four prose pieces that appeared when the volume was published separately. The doggerel whimsy of "To Victor Hugo of My Crow Pluto" must establish some sort of outside limit of the admissible, even for school mistresses. Yet "Tell Me, Tell Me" suggests, at least, that the school mistress is still practicing dippiness according to strategy. I am not sure what this poem is about, but I suspect that it may be about me, about egocentricity that misstates and misunderstands, that ventures to ask why such flatness as "To Victor Hugo of My Crow Pluto" should be set on the cindery pinnacle of publication. The answer is clear: like Mt. Everest, it was there; "it appeared," and in any case "the absorbing geometry of a fantasy" (a short prose piece accompanying the crow poem in the poem's first publications is entitled "My Crow, Pluto—A Fantasy.") is clearly preferable to "grievance touched off on/ any ground," whether hers or mine; "grudges flower less well than gratitudes." [28] Like the coat in that other fantasy by Beatrix Potter, this one is designed "for no tailor-and-cutter jury" but for a few appreciative mice, to whom there is need to say, however deferentially, T. S. V. P. Miss Potter's fantasy "rescued a reader/ from being driven mad by a scold"; perhaps Miss Moore's can do the same. And one must add that she chose this poem to provide the title for the volume in which it appeared.

Such a view of one's writing can be faulted only on grounds that have little relevance to the function the writing serves, thus rendering criticism absurd, as perhaps it is anyway. "Baseball and Writing" not only indicates an apparent switch in loyalties from the Dodgers to the Yankees, but suggests by prescription that "You can never tell with either/ how it will go/ or what you will do" and by example that almost anything associated with your subject may be a part of it. And for readers rescued by this sort of thing, from scolds or whatever, so be it. Thus "Blue Bug" associates a dragon fly, a dancer, a Chinese melody, a dubious etymology, a painter, and an acrobat with a polo pony, the poem's subject. This is, of course, standard procedure for a particular sort of poem, from "Tintern Abbey" to "Among School Children," and the worst that can be said of Miss Moore's example here is that it is not very exciting. The same thing is probably true of "Dream," another fantasy; of "Granite and Steel," another exercise in associations; and of "In Lieu of the Lyre," another wonderfully wobbly statement by the school mistress.

Like fantasies, puzzles may also help to rescue readers. "W. S. Landor" is admirably lucid in its praise of Landor's vigor in dealing with scolds or other undesirables and of his intellectual modesty; "To a Giraffe," leaving its starting point, its subject, and most of its transitions implicit, may or may not deal with the same problems, with the different problem ironically dealt with in "The Mind, Intractable Thing," and with the refuge-hunting in "Tell Me, Tell Me." Thus Landor, "someone I can bear," is clearly not "plagued by the psychological" but remains "less conversational/ than some emotionally tied in knots animal" who talks about anything, even infinity and eternity, but with no real sense of the "consolations of the metaphysical"; if the "journey from sin to redemption" really is perpetual, then why gas about one's personal preferences? It is not really necessary to be a giraffe, perhaps, but there are worse possibilities. Yet the cost of taking one's consolation from the metaphysical rather than letting oneself be plagued by the psychological may be that indicated in "The Mind, Intractable Thing," in which the mind keeps throwing up images but does not tell one how to deal with life or with words. It insists on being both personal and literal (it was memory's eye and ear in "The Mind Is an Enchanting Thing") rather than metaphysical (its human, psychological deformities are opposed, in "Granite and Steel," by the mathematically admirable "'catenary curve' from tower to pier" of the Brooklyn Bridge's cables). Yet it survives, unafraid of just about everything and unregenerately satisfied with its own capacity to make do without those consolations of the metaphysical demanded by fastidiousness in search of a refuge from egocentricity.

Such readings as these strain probability and patience, and I have spoken of *Tell Me, Tell Me* as a mixed grill; yet poem connects with poem. "It isn't jumping around," as Miss Moore once declared of a particularly grasshopperish conversation; "it's all connected." [29] Thus in "An Expedient—Leonardo Da Vinci's—and a Query," Leonardo's patience is a means of dealing with problems that is different from Landor's indignation, but both may provide a kind of refuge, making "great wrongs/ . . . powerless to vex." Perplexing problems bore fruit for Leonardo as for John Roebling, who built the bridge in "Granite and Steel." Leonardo's notebook, with its "flowers, acorns, rocks" exemplifies that "passion for the particular" ascribed to Henry James and Beatrix Potter in "Tell Me, Tell Me." The failure of mathematics to do what Leonardo wanted it to has some troubling relationship with the success of John Roebling's catenary curve and suggests that the consolations of the metaphysical may sometimes be deceptive; at the same time, that failure, opening up a world of which Leonardo could ask "Tell me if anything at all has been done?," suggests deliverance from what "Charity Overcoming Envy" speaks of as an insupportably tiring problem until one realizes that its "Gordian knot need not be cut." Confusion, in such circumstances, becomes retroactive, as in "Old Amusement Park," or as when one has found suitable refuge from egocentricity and its annoying propensities.

"Rescue with Yul Brynner"; "Carnegie Hall: Rescued"; Beatrix Potter's story that "rescued a reader/ from being driven mad by a scold." And in "Saint Valentine," a similar principle of association is specified: things beginning with "v" make appropriate valentine gifts—Vera, her veil, a vignette thereof, bordered by vines and vinelets, verse ("unabashedly bold," the Landor sort), which if written is as the *vendange* to the vine, presumably subjecting the writer to the same proof as the vintage does its grapes. And then the smacking *non sequitur* that egocentricity feels compelled to bisect, mis-state, mis-understand, and obliterate continuity with. As with baseball, "you can never tell . . ./ how it will go/ or what you will do; generating excitement—/ a fever in the victim" of whatever category. And it may take more than an elephant (there is another elephant in "Old Amusement Park"), as in "Charity Overcoming Envy," to "convince . . . the victim/ that Destiny is not devising a plot." Might verse not best confuse itself with Destiny? We may never be sure; very possibly nothing at all has been done, and in any case the Gordian knot need not be cut. But for a committed poet, even one who denies herself the title, verse might very well confuse itself with fate, the final test, for whatever consolation such metaphysical ultimates may afford. And the merest valentine verse is equally as ultimate and unrecallable as "In Distrust of Merits" or "Virginia Britannia," which also begins with "v."

Or as a resurrected poem originally printed in *Contemporary Verse* for January, 1916, under the title "Sun!," then collected in *Observations* as "Fear Is Hope," then as " 'Sun' " in *The Mentor Book of Religious Verse* (1957) ("first published" there, according to the misleading note in *Tell Me, Tell Me*) and *A Marianne Moore Reader*, printed again in the British volume *The Arctic Ox*, and finally coming to rest, without quotation marks, as the last poem in *Tell Me, Tell Me*, half a century later, with persistent minor revision. So located, it has the look of a valedictory poem, an appropriate gesture for one who persistently feels that she may never write again.[30] Cryptic in detail but clear enough in its overall statement, the poem is a sort of Calvinist-Baroque celebration of the Last Judgment, its sun an echo, or anticipation, of the sun that is to shine unfalsifyingly on the sick scene in " 'Keeping Their World Large,' " that both rots and mends in "Efforts of Affection." The God of Michael Wigglesworth and Jonathan Edwards is prefigured in the sun, "a plan/ deep-set within the heart of man," that consumes hostility, whose multiplied flames no insurgent can outrun, and to whose greater glory both holiday and consuming wrath contribute equally in a "device/ of Moorish gorgeousness." This astonishing poem, the work of a woman in her twenties, says, like Eliot's "East Coker" or George Herbert's "Paradise," that our beginnings touch our ends even when they are fifty years apart, and that eschatology is really final.

Four other poems in *Complete Poems* under the heading *Hitherto Uncollected* and a fifth in a recent *New Yorker* ("Mercifully," July 20, 1968, p. 34) indicate that Miss Moore continues to write. None of the five seem particularly compelling, though "Love in America" demonstrates a capacity to be wryly amused by something that, on the whole, she approves of as at least better than nay-saying. "I've Been Thinking" will probably prompt little of that process in a reader, and "The Camperdown Elm" comes dangerously close to burlesque of its intentions, though the dippy school mistress may be the only one who can save the tree. "Tippoo's Tiger" reads like notes for a poem in need of putting together, a ballad that "still awaits a tiger-hearted bard"; and "Mercifully," following the lead of "Tell Me, Tell Me," finds in music a refuge from pretentiousness and impercipience. Small things, but not dishonorable or presumptuous.

"Poetry," wrote Miss Moore at seventy-one, "is the Mogul's dream: to be intensively toiling at what is a pleasure. . . . As for the hobgoblin obscurity, it need never entail compromise. It should mean that one may fail and start again, never mutilate an auspicious premise. The objective is architecture, not demolition; grudges flower less well than gratitudes. To shape, to shear, compress, and delineate; to 'add a hue to the spectrum of another's mind' as Mark Van Doren has enhanced the poems of Thomas Hardy, should make it difficult for anyone to dislike poetry!"[31] Her claims here are modest, excessively so for some of her work of the thirties and forties, poems which constitute part of the moral intelligence of our time. But they do very well—one can say it without condescension—for the late work of one who, in Robert Lowell's words, "never said a commonplace thing in her life."[32]

CHAPTER 7

The Rock Crystal Thing to See

"Miss Moore's poems," wrote W. H. Auden, "are an example of a kind of art which is not as common as it should be; they delight, not only because they are intelligent, sensitive and beautifully written, but also because they convince the reader that they have been written by someone who is personally good." [1] Wallace Stevens wrote of her in a 1953 letter, "How good she is as compared to most literary people! None of the egotism and nerves. . . ." [2] Bernard Engel quotes William Carlos Williams on her role in the group associated with Alfred Kreymborg just prior to 1920: she "was our saint. . . . Everyone loved her." [3] And in an age that Randall Jarrell has memorably identified as one of criticism, a criticism that "might just as well have been written by a syndicate of encyclopedias for an audience of International Business Machines," [4] such unabashed concern for a person rings oddly. Milton might believe "that he who would not be frustrate of his hope to write well hereafter in laudable things, ought himself to be a true poem, that is, a composition and pattern of the best and honorablest things," [5] but both the phrasing and the idea are likely to strike most twentieth-century readers as naïve.

Auden's observation is thus startling; but it may also be accurate, a useful index not just of Miss Moore's capacity for inspiring personal affection but of both the characteristic excitements and the characteristic limitations of her poems. Limitations are, on the whole, easier to describe than excitements, and the point I have in mind here may again be documented out of Milton, the passage from "Areopagitica," already quoted in Chapter 5,[6] on the inseparability of good and evil in this world. Over thirty years ago, R. P. Blackmur remarked that "the poem 'Marriage,' an excellent poem, is never concerned with either love or lust, but with something else, perhaps no less valuable, but certainly, in a profound sense, less complete," and "in Miss Moore life is remote (life as good *and* evil) and everything is done to keep it remote." [7] Writing in 1935, Blackmur could not have concerned himself with "In Distrust of Merits," but Randall Jarrell, writing some fifteen years later, could, and Jarrell echoes Blackmur's reservation: "The way of the little jerboa on the sands—at once true, beautiful, and good—she understands; but the little shrew or weasel, that kills, if it can, two or three dozen animals in a night?" [8] and again, "poems which celebrate morality choose more between good and evil, and less between lesser evils and greater goods, than life does, so that in them morality is simpler and more beautiful than it is in life, and we feel our attachment to it strengthened." [9] Fifty years ago Miss Moore anticipated such comments: "I will not touch or have to do with those things which I detest";[10] and her 1960 comment on Allen Ginsberg (he "can foul the nest in a way to marvel at, but it is an innocent enough picture of himself which he provides when he 'sat down under the huge shade of a Southern Pacific locomotive'"[11]) suggests a degree of mellowing, perhaps, but no fundamental change.

The suggestion is, of course, misleading, but in a special way. Miss Moore knows that the world is not good and evil but good-and-evil, as her ironic sense of man in "Virginia Britannia," "The Pangolin," and "Armor's Undermining Modesty" makes clear; she knows that Marianne Moore is not good or evil but good-and-evil, as "In Distrust of Merits" and "A Face" make equally clear. But reticence, decorum, propriety, an unwillingness to foul the nest in however marvelous a way, or perhaps a mere choice of subject matter operate to hold such knowledge at arm's length; not for her Yeats's descent into the foul rag and bone shop of the heart or Rilke's discovery of existence in Baudelaire's *"Une Charogne."* One is not tempted to say that Yeats's poems "convince the reader that they have been written by someone who is personally good." Virtue, rectitude—Miss Moore's work shines with them, but an ideologue might be forgiven for murmuring, "Bourgeois virtue, bourgeois rectitude." "Art," she writes, "is but an expression of our needs."[12] Perhaps one of our deepest needs—politically, morally, personally—is the clear sense of our capacity for reversion, of the inadequacy of our good intentions, of what Auden himself identified in "The Cave of Making":

> More than ever
> life-out-there is goodly, miraculous, lovable,
>   but we shan't, not since Stalin and Hitler,
> trust ourselves ever again: we know that, subjectively,
>   all is possible.[13]

The abandoned "Melancthon," once more, wonders what life

will be "to one who can see no/ beautiful element of unreason under it." But equally, if somewhat unfairly, the question might concern itself with one who sees no threat in that beautiful element of unreason, and the answer would have to be, "admirable but incomplete." Of the Georgian poets, David Daiches remarks that they "seem to have their eyes averted from something";[14] and Marianne Moore, praising moderate heroes, constructing her moralized bestiary, upholding fastidiousness in small things and integrity in large— manifesting, in fact, personal goodness, a daily beauty that needs no defense—leaves a similar impression as part of the cost of her way of art.

What else does it leave? What are the characteristic excitements of that way of art? Tricky prosody contributes something, as do the sometimes astringent wit and the capacity for an almost pedantically precise, and therefore surprising and amusing, observation. Beyond this, one goes cautiously, more aware of what is not conspicuously there than of what is. One is not aware especially of a philosophy, a point of view; one does not especially value her work as a matter of historical interest, a document of its time, like *Ulysses* or *The Cantos*. In spite of the clear sense in which Miss Moore's is an intellectual poetry, it is not really a poetry of ideas, in the sense that Yeats's or Eliot's or Stevens' is. Nor does it have much dramatic interest, still less the intensely "confessional" interest of Robert Lowell, Theodore Roethke, or Anne Sexton, for whom, as for Eliot and Yeats in their different manners, the modern world's existential human anguish is subject.

There is, in fact, a sense in which Miss Moore is not especially modern, not of the twentieth century, except in incidentals and superficials. This recognition appears brilliantly in Robert Payne's fine tour de force "On Mariamna De Maura," in which Miss Moore is translated into a vaguely fourteenth- or fifteenth-century prodigy, published first by Aldus Manutius in 1489, sought after for her conversation by the Pope, moving among dragons and meteors with an easy grace.[15] Jean Garrigue notes resemblances with Emily Dickinson.[16] And one might develop the notion that her emphasis on decorum and propriety suggests less our own time than the eighteenth century, that great and mistaken century in which it was almost possible to believe that man was capable of living reasonably. And I suspect that a chief source of excitement in Miss Moore's work looks toward that point at which the eighteenth century flowed into the nineteenth, in the person of Wordsworth, who subtitled his most ambitious poem "Growth of a Poet's Mind."

In an earlier chapter, I suggested ambiguity in the lines from "The Hero,"

> He's not out
> seeing a sight but the rock
> crystal thing to see,

which can mean either "he's out seeing the rock crystal thing to see" or "he is the rock crystal thing to see." [17] If we take this as inclusive rather than exclusive ambiguity, on the analogy of Hopkins' notorious "buckle" in "The Windhover," then the hero is out looking at himself; the hero's grasp of reality, like Wordsworth's, expresses itself in the gesture of Narcissus. And though Miss Moore nowhere tells us that the hero is the poet, much less that it is she, still the image is an apt one for the subjects and procedures of her poems. What is a Marianne Moore poem about? It is about the odd and interesting way Marianne Moore's mind works as it moves from object to object and from aspect to aspect. "Everything zigzags in this poetry," [18] says Marguerite Young. What attracts Miss Moore, and us, is her mind's very uncertainness, its unpredictable capacity to associate—"the manner in which we associate ideas in a state of excitement," as Wordsworth put it in the preface to *Lyrical Ballads*.[19]

For Miss Moore, such associations sometimes approach Wordsworth's experience in the Wye valley near Tintern Abbey, discovering what he did not know he knew—that things have life, that we share in an organically continuous whole, that there is something in existence far more deeply interfused even than the still, sad music of humanity. But Miss Moore's discoveries are characteristically smaller; she knows that the theater she looks into is not the living plenum Wordsworth saw but her own quirky consciousness. For Wordsworth, poetry was "the first and last of all knowledge";[20] for Miss Moore, it is at best the Mogul's dream, at worst, fiddle. For Wordsworth, poetry had as its object "truth, not individual and local, but general and operative; not standing upon external testimony, but carried alive into the heart by passion; truth which is its own testimony, which gives completeness and confidence to the tribunal to which it appeals, and receives them from the same tribunal." [21] It is a measure both of similarity and of difference that Miss Moore could say much the same thing; the real toad in the imaginary garden is, in its small way, a Wordsworthian truth.

The way is smaller. Unlike the romantics, Miss Moore

has never overvalued poetry. The great phrases in which they talked of poetry and the poet—Wordsworth's "breath and finer spirit of all knowledge," [22] Shelley's "unacknowledged legislators of the world" [23]—have little to do with the woman who said of poetry, "I, too, dislike it," and would like to have invented the zipper fastener or epoxy glue.[24] Wordsworth, watching his mind at work, could believe that he was fulfilling the wisdom and spirit of the universe; the ascent of Mt. Snowdon in the last book of *The Prelude* was also an ascent to truth, that spoke to him not of himself but of a mind that feeds upon infinity. Miss Moore, like Pope and with something of his capacity for self-irony, stoops to truth, speaking of a mind that is often enchanting, sometimes intractable, but never nobly vague, never pinnacled dim in the intense inane.

She may also touch Wordsworth at one other point, the Wordsworth who, betrayed by the French Revolution and by himself, "yielded up moral questions in despair," [25] then found in his slow recovery the matter and motive for his finest work—a process described by Robert Langbaum as one whereby "men of genius arrived intellectually at the dead-end of the eighteenth century and then, often through a total crisis of personality, broke intellectually into the nineteenth." [26] "In Distrust of Merits" gives us crisis, the poems that follow it in *Collected Poems* give us convalescence and recovery.[27] Perhaps it is excessive to detect in Miss Moore a "total crisis of personality," but we know that Wordsworth tells us all, whereas she understates; perhaps it is extravagant to find Miss Moore arriving at an intellectual dead-end and breaking into a different world, but Langbaum notes repetition of Wordsworth's crisis "in at least three generations thereafter." [28] As Charles Williams reminds us,[29] Wordsworth's crisis occurred in his twenties, preceding all his characteristic poetry; Miss Moore had already developed her characteristic manner and preoccupations by the time of *What Are Years?* and *Nevertheless.* Even had she wished, recasting herself into a different mold to meet the experiences of the late 1930s and the 1940s would have been a monumental and perhaps impossible undertaking, though something relevant to such recasting may be expressed in her persistent revising and rearranging of her work; and one recalls again her persistent consideration of that work as something less than poetry. Once more, the scale is smaller than Wordsworth's, as the manner is more idiosyncratic.

But once more, what Wordsworth gives us at his best is a mind in its operations—its growth, he was assured, into a mature wisdom that was to have resulted in *The Recluse.* *The Recluse* was never written; we have instead the "Ecclesiastical Sonnets," in which the mind has ceased to operate in the old way, merely giving results instead. Miss Moore proposed less, in fact, proposed nothing. "As someone said in the foreword to an exhibition catalogue of his work, 'With what shall the artist arm himself save with his humility?' Humility, indeed, is armor, for it realizes that it is impossible to be original, in the sense of doing something that has never been thought of before." [30] Humility may be excessive, as may a concern for armor, though there is little to gain from speculating on the imaginable work of a humble Wordsworth or an egotistically sublime Marianne Moore. Nor is there really any need. Marianne Moore's mind, whether walking along with its eyes on the ground or being rebuked for its deformities by John Roebling's catenary curve, grinding its own ax, dealing with pent-up emotion, or wishing it had invented the zipper, is at the very least a worthy counterpart of the Camperdown elm, one of our crowning curios. And Marianne Moore, armored with humility, might well take that to be quite enough.

As perhaps it is. Yet epigrammatic brilliance, intellectual fastidiousness, and an unwillingness to falsify one's sense of one's own limitations may have an exemplary value of their own, in art as well as in life. Marianne Moore does not tell us the meaning of history, the nature of sin, or the right way to conduct our lives. She keeps thing in order; she observes and annotates; she exercises the courage of her peculiarities. She gives us imaginary gardens with real toads in them; she also gives us the sick horror of decency trying to confront honestly the fact of modern war, and the undramatic, faintly humiliating, matter-of-fact discovery that decency recovers from that confrontation. Without heroics and without chatter, she tells us that "originality is . . . a by-product of sincerity" [31]—that is, a moral phenomenon, like Pavlova's dancing[32] —and for half a century now she has been demonstrating what that means. As she wrote of Eliot, "The effect of [such] confidences, elucidations, and precepts . . . is to disgust us with affectation; to encourage respect for spiritual humility; and to encourage us to do our ardent undeviating best with the medium in which we work." [33] Auden was right; in reading Miss Moore, one responds as much to a person as to a work. Auden's comment in a poem "on the occasion of her eightieth birthday, November 15, 1967," sums up both:

> "How well and with what unfreckled integrity
> It has all been done." [34]

Notes

Chapter 1. Some Question of Integrity

1. Bernard F. Engel, *Marianne Moore*, p. 30.
2. Marianne Moore, "Interview with Donald Hall," *A Marianne Moore Reader*, p. 258.
3. James D. Hart, *The Oxford Companion to American Literature*, p. 193.
4. *Reader*, pp. 221–22.
5. Monroe Wheeler, "Reminiscence," *Festschrift for Marianne Moore's Seventy Seventh Birthday*, ed. M. J. Tambimuttu, p. 128.
6. Quoted in Tambimuttu, "Instead of a Preface," *Festschrift*, p. 15. On the number of r's in "error," see Marianne Moore, "The Pangolin," *The Complete Poems of Marianne Moore*, p. 119.
7. *The Letters of Hart Crane*, ed. Brom Weber, p. 289.
8. *The Letters of Ezra Pound*, ed. D. D. Paige, p. 295.
9. "Subject, Predicate, Object," *Tell Me, Tell Me*, p. 46.
10. "The Ways Our Poets Have Taken Since the War," *Reader*, p. 240.
11. Winthrop Sargeant, "Humility, Concentration, and Gusto," *The New Yorker*, XXXII (Feb. 16, 1957), 70.
12. Donald Hall, "Interview with Marianne Moore," *McCall's*, XCIII (Dec., 1965), 74, 182.
13. Quoted by George Plimpton, "The World Series with Marianne Moore," *Harper's*, CCXXIX (Oct., 1964), 52–53.
14. "Brooklyn from Clinton Hill," *Reader*, p. 183.
15. *Letters of Wallace Stevens*, ed. Holly Stevens, p. 737.

16. *Selected Poems*, p. 108.
17. *Collected Poems*, p. 5.
18. "Interview," *Reader*, p. 256.
19. *Ibid.*, p. 265.
20. *Ibid.*, p. 256.
21. *Ibid.*, p. 258.
22. *Ibid.*
23. Strictly speaking, *Observations* is her third book, since the poem "Marriage" was printed in 1923 as a stapled pamphlet.
24. "*The Dial*: A Retrospect," *Predilections*, p. 104.
25. "Interview," *Reader*, pp. 258–59.
26. *Ibid.*, p. 267.
27. *Literary and Library Prizes*, ed. Olga S. Weber, p. 12.
28. Lewis Nichols, "Talk with Marianne Moore," *The New York Times Book Review*, May 16, 1954, p. 30.
29. Sargeant, "Humility, Concentration, and Gusto," *The New Yorker*, XXXII (Feb. 16, 1957), 64.
30. "Interview," *Reader*, p. 264.
31. Hugh Kenner, "Supreme in Her Abnormality," *Poetry: A Magazine of Verse*, LXXXIV (Sept., 1954), 356.
32. Weber, *Literary and Library Prizes*, p. 178.
33. Hall, "Interview with Marianne Moore," *McCall's*, XCIII (Dec., 1965), 190.
34. Jane Howard, "Leading Lady of U.S. Verse," *Life*, LXII (Jan. 13, 1967), p. 42.
35. "MacDowell Colony, 50 Years Old, Hails Marianne Moore," *The New York Times*, Aug. 21, 1967, p. 33M.
36. "Miss Moore in Manhattan," *The New Yorker*, LXI (Jan. 29, 1966), 26.
37. Howard, "Leading Lady of U.S. Verse," *Life*, LXII (Jan. 13, 1967), 40.
38. Engel, *Marianne Moore*, pp. 39–40.
39. Sargeant, "Humility, Concentration, and Gusto," *The New Yorker*, XXXII (Feb. 16, 1957), 48.

40. Plimpton, "The World Series with Marianne Moore," *Harper's*, CCXXIX (Oct., 1964), 52.
41. *Ibid.*, p. 55.
42. Howard, "Leading Lady of U.S. Verse," *Life*, LXII (Jan. 13, 1967), 40.
43. Stevens, *Letters of Wallace Stevens*, p. 756.
44. Howard, "Leading Lady of U.S. Verse," *Life*, LXII (Jan. 13, 1967), 40.
45. Sargeant, "Humility, Concentration, and Gusto," *The New Yorker*, XXXII (Feb. 16, 1957), 49.

Chapter 2. The Courage of Our Peculiarities

1. Marianne Moore, "Feeling and Precision," *Predilections*, p. 3.
2. *Ibid.*, p. 6.
3. "A Burning Desire To Be Explicit," *Christian Science Monitor*, Jan. 11, 1966, p. 12; reprinted, with modifications, in *Tell Me, Tell Me.*
4. "Interview with Donald Hall," *A Marianne Moore Reader*, p. 258.
5. *Complete Poems*, p. 267.
6. Randall Jarrell, "Her Shield," *Poetry and the Age*, p. 191.
7. *Collected Poems*, p. 48; not reprinted in *Complete Poems.*
8. "Things Others Never Notice," *Predilections*, p. 138.
9. Hugh Kenner, "Meditation and Enactment," *Poetry: A Magazine of Verse*, CII (May, 1963), 110.
10. "Besitz und Gemeingut," *Predilections*, p. 121.
11. Charles Tomlinson, "Abundance, Not Too Much: The Poetry of Marianne Moore," *Sewanee Review*, LXV (Autumn, 1957), 677.
12. *Predilections*, p. 3; see above, p. 16.
13. "Humility, Concentration, and Gusto," *Predilections*, p. 15.
14. "Poetry," *Complete Poems*, pp. 266–67.

15. "Picking and Choosing," *Collected Poems*, p. 52; the passage has been revised in *Complete Poems*.
16. If "it" in the next-to-last line refers to "sea" rather than "art," then this reading will not stand; but then it becomes virtually impossible to make sense of the passage.
17. "Feeling and Precision," *Predilections*, p. 11.
18. Winthrop Sargeant, "Humility, Concentration, and Gusto," *The New Yorker*, XXXII (Feb. 16, 1957), 72.
19. "Profit Is a Dead Weight," *Tell Me, Tell Me*, p. 22.
20. *Predilections*, p. 3; see above, p. 16.
21. The elephants have their moment in "Melancthon," immediately following "The Monkeys" in *Collected Poems*; and the monkeys' shortcomings (they "winked too much and were afraid of snakes") get some attention three poems later in "Picking and Choosing": "Literature is a phase of life. If one is afraid of it,/ the situation is irremediable." And Miss Moore adds, "if one approaches it familiarly/ what one says of it is worthless," which may have bearing on the cat's positiveness.
22. "Feeling and Precision," *Predilections*, p. 11.
23. "Anna Pavlova," *Predilections*, pp. 154–55.
24. *The Selected Letters of John Keats*, ed. Lionel Trilling, p. 243.
25. "Religion and the Intellectuals," *Partisan Review*, XVII (Feb., 1950), 137.
26. "Interview," *Reader*, p. 253.
27. Sargeant, "Humility, Concentration, and Gusto," *The New Yorker*, XXXII (Feb. 16, 1967), 42.
28. "Feeling and Precision," *Predilections*, pp. 7–8.
29. "Interview," *Reader*, p. 259.
30. R. P. Blackmur, "The Method of Marianne Moore," *Language as Gesture*, p. 281.
31. "Interview," *Reader*, p. 263.
32. *Ibid.*
33. "Humility, Concentration, and Gusto," *Predilections*, p. 20.
34. "It Is Not Forbidden to Think," *Predilections*, p. 50.
35. "Every Shadow a Friend," *Predilections*, p. 146.

36. "Selected Criticism," *Reader*, p. 232.
37. Above, p. 21.
38. *Complete Poems*, p. 266.
39. *Observations*, p. 31.
40. Blackmur, "The Method of Marianne Moore," *Language as Gesture*, pp. 269–70.
41. Above, p. 35.
42. *Poems* (London, 1921), p. 22; this version was first printed in *Others*, V (July, 1919), 5, and reprinted by Alfred Kreymborg in his anthology *Others for 1919* (New York, 1920), pp. 131–32.
43. *Poems*, p. 16.

Chapter 3. Additions and Subtractions

1. "To a Chameleon," noted on p. 60, and "I May, I Might, I Must," which appeared in Bryn Mawr's literary magazine *Tipyn O'Bob* in June, 1909, under the title "Progress."
2. See Eugene P. Sheehy and Kenneth A. Lohf, *The Achievement of Marianne Moore: A Bibliography, 1907–1957*, pp. 11–16.
3. Joseph Warren Beach, *The Making of the Auden Canon.*
4. See *Poetry: A Magazine of Verse*, VII (Nov., 1915), 81–83; and *The Collected Poems of Wallace Stevens*, pp. 66–70.
5. *Letters of Wallace Stevens*, ed. Holly Stevens, p. 183.
6. Above, pp. 35–41.
7. "Refinement" in line three was "fineness," "because" in line four was "by virtue," and "Complexity" in line fourteen was "A complexity."
8. See above, p. 29.
9. See above pp. 27–28. 34–35.
10. "Subject, Predicate, Object," *Tell Me, Tell Me*, p. 46; see above, p. 2.
11. *The Collected Poetry of W. H. Auden*, p. vii.
12. As with this poem, Miss Moore's titles are sometimes part of the first sentence and must be read accordingly.

13. *Observations,* p. 24.
14. T. S. Eliot, *Four Quartets,* p. 13.
15. "A Burning Desire To Be Explicit," *Tell Me, Tell Me,* p. 5.
16. *The Selected Letters of John Keats,* ed. Lionel Trilling, p. 257.
17. Jonah 4.4.
18. *Ibid.,* 4.8.
19. Randall Jarrell, "Her Shield," *Poetry and the Age,* p. 192.
20. "Religion and the Intellectuals," *Partisan Review,* XVII (Feb., 1950), 137.
21. Quoted by William Wasserstrom, "Marianne Moore's *Dial,*" *Festschrift for Marianne Moore's Seventy Seventh Birthday,* ed. M. J. Tambimuttu, pp. 35–36.
22. Allen Tate, in *Festschrift,* ed. Tambimuttu, p. 113.
23. "*The Dial*: A Retrospect," *Predilections,* p. 114.
24. "Subject, Predicate, Object," *Tell Me, Tell Me,* p. 48.
25. Jarrell, "Her Shield," *Poetry and the Age,* p. 196.
26. *Ibid.,* p. 206.
27. Stevens, *Letters of Wallace Stevens,* p. 737.
28. *Ibid.,* p. 715.
29. W. H. Auden, "Marianne Moore," *The Dyer's Hand and Other Essays,* p. 305.
30. *Ibid.,* pp. 298–99.

Chapter 4. Intelligence in Its Pure Form

1. See above, p. 46.
2. "Both ["In Distrust of Merits" and " 'Keeping Their World Large' "] attempt to deal with the theme of war and both fail because the feeling is no longer contained." Charles Tomlinson, "Abundance, Not Too Much: The Poetry of Marianne Moore," *Sewanee Review,* LXV (Autumn, 1957), 685.
3. Robert Penn Warren, "Jingle: In Tribute to a Great Poem by Marianne Moore," *Festschrift for Marianne Moore's Seventy-Seventh Birthday,* ed. M. J. Tambimuttu, p. 103.

4. "Interview with Donald Hall," *A Marianne Moore Reader*, p. 261.

5. *Observations* appears to have been put together in straight chronological order, though the evidence provided by dates of initial publication is tenuous at best. My group three are the last poems in the book, and the sequence from "In the Days of Prismatic Color" through "Sea Unicorns and Land Unicorns" is as in *Complete Poems*, with the exception of "Silence" and one omitted poem, "Dock Rats."

6. Samuel Johnson, "Cowley," *The Lives of the Most Eminent English Poets*, ed. W. E. Henley, I, 14.

7. *The Selected Letters of John Keats*, ed. Lionel Thrilling, p. 101.

8. "Subject, Predicate, Object," *Tell Me, Tell Me*, p. 48; see above, p. 70.

9. Monroe Wheeler, "Reminiscence," *Festschrift*, ed. Tambimuttu), p. 129.

10. Randall Jarrell, "Her Shield," *Poetry and the Age*, p. 191; see above, p. 19.

11. Johnson, "Cowley," *The Lives of the Most Eminent English Poets*, I, 13.

12. Regarding yellow roses, Marguerite Young reports Miss Moore's recollection that her mother's garden in Carlisle, Pennsylvania, contained only yellow flowers. And Miss Young adds a characteristic note regarding Miss Moore's persistent attachment to particulars; in the Carlisle garden "there was a brick with a cat's paws marked in it . . . she arose and left the room and came back with the brick in her hand." Marguerite Young, "An Afternoon with Marianne Moore," *Festschrift*, ed. Tambimuttu), p. 69.

13. A. Kingsley Weatherhead, *The Edge of the Image: Marianne Moore, William Carlos Williams, and Some Other Poets*, p. 69.

14. Frederika Beatty, *William Wordsworth of Dove Cottage*, p. 30.

15. R. P. Blackmur, "The Method of Marianne Moore," *Language as Gesture*, p. 271.

16. Bernard F. Engel, *Marianne Moore*, p. 58.
17. Chapter 19; in the Garnett translation it is not pots but bricks.
18. Elizabeth Hardwick, "Boston: The Lost Ideal," *Harper's*, CCXIX (Dec., 1959), 67.
19. Jarrell, "The Humble Animal," *Poetry and the Age*, p. 182.
20. *The Letters of Ezra Pound*, ed. D. D. Paige, p. 295; see above, p. 2.
21. Siegfried Sassoon, "On Reading the War Diary of a Defunct Ambassador," *Collected Poems of Siegfried Sassoon*, p. 130.
22. See above, pp. 79–82.
23. Marianne Moore, "Feeling and Precision," *Predilections*, p. 11; see above, pp. 25–26, 27.
24. Above, pp. 50–51.
25. Above, pp. 21–22.
26. Above, pp. 44–45.
27. "Marriage" also has the distinction of being the first, and for twenty-five years the only, poem of Miss Moore's to receive separate publication—by Monroe Wheeler in 1923, as *Manikin Number Three*.
28. William Carlos Williams, "Prologue to *Kora in Hell*," *Selected Essays of William Carlos Williams*, p. 7.
29. Young, "An Afternoon with Marianne Moore," *Festschrift*, ed. Tambimuttu, p. 70.
30. "Subject, Predicate, Object," *Tell Me, Tell Me*, p. 46.
31. George Bernard Shaw, *Man and Superman*, p. 214.
32. William Wasserstrom, "Irregular Symmetry: Marianne Moore's *Dial*," *Festschrift*, ed. Tambimuttu, p. 37.
33. Above, p. 7.
34. *"The Dial:* A Retrospect," *Predilections*, p. 106.
35. *Ibid.*, pp. 103–104.
36. "Interview," *Reader*, p. 266.
37. *Ibid.*, p. 268.

Chapter 5. The Other Voice

1. Above, p. 46.
2. T. D. Barlow, *Woodcuts of Albrecht Dürer*, p. 19.
3. Wallace Stevens, *The Collected Poems of Wallace Stevens*, p. 250.
4. "Conjuries That Endure," *Predilections*, p. 39.
5. *Ibid.*, p. 36.
6. Bernard F. Engel, *Marianne Moore*, p. 45.
7. *Ibid.*, p. 47.
8. A. Kingsley Weatherhead, *The Edge of the Image: Marianne Moore, William Carlos William, and Some Other Poets*, p. 88.
9. Roy Harvey Pearce, *The Continuity of American Poetry*, p. 372.
10. "Anna Pavlova," *Predilections*, p. 147.
11. "Subject, Predicate, Object," *Tell Me, Tell Me*, p. 48.
12. "If I Were Sixteen Today," *A Marianne Moore Reader*, p. 196.
13. Winthrop Sargeant, "Humility, Concentration, and Gusto," *The New Yorker*, XXXII (Feb. 16, 1957), p. 42.
14. The notes to this poem are confusing, including as they do references to a giant tame armadillo and some red-spotted orchids that appear in the pre-*Collected Poems* versions but were subsequently revised out. Similar anomalies are preserved in the notes to "Nine Nectarines."
15. Robert Penn Warren, "Jingle: In Tribute to a Great Poem by Marianne Moore," *Festschrift for Marianne Moore's Seventy Seventh Birthday*, ed. M. J. Tambimuttu, p. 103.
16. Oscar Williams, ed., *New Poems 1940*, p. 9.
17. *Ibid.*, p. 13.
18. *What Are Years?* in fact itself repeats the pattern of *Selected Poems* and its components as described at the beginning of the preceding chapter. In 1936 Miss Moore published *The Pangolin and Other Verse*, a twenty-four-page, one-hundred-twenty-copy limited edition of five previously uncollected poems; *What Are Years?* consists of the contents of *The Pangolin and Other*

Verse and other, later things. For whatever reason, it is also the last of the separate collections to have been substantially altered for its reprinting in *Collected Poems* and *Complete Poems*, three poems of its original fifteen having been abandoned—"Walking-Sticks and Paper-Weights and Water Marks," "Half Deity," and "See in the Midst of Fair Leaves."

19. W. H. Auden, "Making, Knowing and Judging," *The Dyer's Hand and Other Essays*, p. 51.

20. *The Collected Poetry of W. H. Auden*, p. 198.

21. *The Collected Poems of W. B. Yeats*, p. 291.

22. Lionel Trilling, "The Immortality Ode," *The Liberal Imagination*, p. 151.

23. Pearce, *The Continuity of American Poetry*, p. 372; see above, p. 115.

24. C. S. Lewis, "Edmund Spenser," *Major British Writers* (ed. G. B. Harrison), I, 101.

25. "If I Were Sixteen Today," *Reader*, p. 197.

26. *Ibid.*, p. 195.

27. "September 1, 1939," in Williams, *New Poems 1940*, p. 28.

28. Kimon Friar and John Malcolm Brinnin, eds., *Modern Poetry*, p. 523.

29. See above, pp. 79–81.

30. Above, p. 76.

31. "Interview with Donald Hall," *Reader*, p. 261.

32. Weatherhead, *The Edge of the Image*, pp. 81–82.

33. Randall Jarrell, "The Humble Animal," *Poetry and the Age*, p. 183.

34. Here, as elsewhere, poems seem to be arranged on other than chronological principles, if we may judge on the basis of first publication dates. The nine poems show the following sequence, by years: 1947, 1948, 1950, 1944, 1944, 1948, 1947, 1944, 1950. Once more, the sequence seems to be strategic rather than mechanical.

35. "Selected Criticism," *Reader*, pp. 230–31.

36. Louise Bogan, *Selected Criticism: Prose, Poetry*.

37. Quoted by J. B. Leishman in Rainer Maria Rilke, *Duino Elegies*, tr. J. B. Leishman and Stephen Spender, p. 101.
38. *Ibid.*, p. 33.
39. *Ibid.*
40. *Ibid.*, p. 27.
41. Wallace Fowlie, "Marianne Moore," *Sewanee Review*, LX (July, 1952), 538.
42. "Selected Criticism," *Reader*, p. 231.
43. "Interview," *Reader*, p. 262.
44. I do not know what, if any, actual correspondence may exist between Miss Moore's private life and the suggestions of spiritual crisis deducible from these poems, nor does there seem to be any decent way of finding out. Mrs. Moore's death can hardly have been easy for her daughter, however, and, for what it may be worth, Wallace Stevens wrote to Norman Holmes Pearson on January 24, 1952, six weeks after the American publication of Miss Moore's *Collected Poems*: "The truth is that I am much moved by what she is going through. It is easy to say that Marianne, the human being, does not concern us. *Mais, mon Dieu*, it is what concerns us most." *Letters of Wallace Stevens*, p. 737.
45. *Complete Poems* omits line three from stanza three of the version of " 'Keeping Their World Large' " that was printed in *Collected Poems*: "When the very heart was a prayer."
46. Jarrell, "Her Shield," *Poetry and the Age*, p. 204.
47. John Milton, "Areopagitica," *Complete Prose Works of John Milton*, ed. D. Bush et al. II, 514.

Chapter 6. The Mogul's Dream

1. See above, p. 9.
2. Donald Hall, "Interview with Marianne Moore," *McCall's*, XCIII (Dec., 1965), 190; see above, p. 12.
3. "Interview with Donald Hall," *A Marianne Moore Reader*, p. 256.

4. *Ibid.*, p. 259.

5. "Subject, Predicate, Object," *Tell Me, Tell Me*, p. 47.

6. Randall Jarrell, "Her Shield," *Poetry and the Age*, p. 189.

7. See below, pp. 157–158.

8. Letter to Marianne Moore from Robert B. Young of Ford's Marketing Research Division, "The Ford Correspondence," *Reader*, pp. 215–16.

9. See above, Chapter 3.

10. David Daiches, *Poetry and the Modern World*, p. 189.

11. T. D. Barlow, *Woodcuts of Albrecht Dürer*, plate 101.

12. Winthrop Sargeant, "Humility, Concentration, and Gusto," *The New Yorker*, XXXII (Feb. 16, 1957), 42.

13. *Ibid.*, pp. 66–70.

14. "Foreword," *Reader*, p. xv.

15. *Ibid.*, pp. xvi–xvii; see also "Idiosyncrasy and Technique," *Reader*, pp. 175–77.

16. "Interview," *Reader*, p. 261.

17. Above, p. 151.

18. Hugh Kenner, "Meditation and Enactment," *Poetry: A Magazine of Verse*, CII (May, 1963), 111.

19. See above, pp. 64–67.

20. "Religion and the Intellectuals," *Partisan Review*, XVII (Feb., 1950), 137.

21. "Silence."

22. This reading of "In the Public Garden" owes much to that of A. Kingsley Weatherhead, *The Edge of the Image: Marianne Moore, William Carlos Williams, and Some Other Poets*, pp. 74–77.

23. "Reticent Candor," *Reader*, p. 142.

24. Matt. 18.3.

25. See Weatherhead, *The Edge of the Image*, pp. 39–42.

26. *Ibid.*, p. 73.

27. Bernard F. Engel, *Marianne Moore*, p. 150.

28. "Subject, Predicate, Object," *Tell Me, Tell Me*, p. 48.

29. Sargeant, "Humility, Concentration, and Gusto," *The New Yorker*, XXXII (Feb. 16, 1957), 48.
30. See above, pp. 147–148.
31. "Subject, Predicate, Object," *Tell Me, Tell Me*, p. 49.
32. Quoted by M. J. Tambimuttu, "Instead of a Preface," *Festschrift for Marianne Moore's Seventy Seventh Birthday*, ed. M. J. Tambimuttu, p. 15.

Chapter 7. The Rock Crystal Thing to See

1. W. H. Auden, "Marianne Moore," *The Dyer's Hand and Other Essays*, p. 305; see above, p. 73.
2. *Letters of Wallace Stevens*, ed. Holly Stevens, p. 772.
3. Bernard F. Engel, *Marianne Moore*, p. 33.
4. Randall Jarrell, "The Age of Criticism," *Poetry and the Age*, pp. 72–73.
5. John Milton, "An Apology for a Pamphlet," *Complete Prose Works of John Milton*, ed. Douglas Bush et al., I, 890.
6. Above, pp. 145–146.
7. R. P. Blackmur, "The Method of Marianne Moore," *Language as Gesture*, pp. 283–84.
8. Jarrell, "Her Shield," *Poetry and the Age*, p. 198.
9. *Ibid.*, p. 185.
10. William Carlos Williams, "Prologue to *Kora in Hell*," *Selected Essays of William Carlos Williams*, p. 7.
11. "The Ways Our Poets Have Taken Since the War," *A Marianne Moore Reader*, p. 240.
12. "Feeling and Precision," *Predilections*, p. 11; see above, p. 25.
13. W. H. Auden, *About the House*, p. 9.
14. David Daiches, *Poetry and the Modern World*, p. 46.
15. Robert Payne, "On Mariamna De Maura," *Festschrift for Marianne Moore's Seventy Seventh Birthday*, ed. M. J. Tambimuttu, pp. 21–27.

16. Jean Garrigue, "Emily Dickinson, Marianne Moore," *Festschrift*, ed. Tambimuttu, pp. 52–57.

17. See above, pp. 113–114.

18. Marguerite Young, "An Afternoon with Marianne Moore," *Festschrift*, ed. Tambimuttu, p. 66.

19. *The Poetical Works of William Wordsworth*, ed. Thomas Hutchinson, p. 935.

20. *Ibid.*, p. 939.

21. *Ibid.*, p. 938.

22. *Ibid.*

23. *The Complete Works of Percy Bysshe Shelley*, ed. Roger Ingpen and Walter E. Peck, VII, 140.

24. "Profit Is a Dead Weight," *Tell Me, Tell Me*, p. 22.

25. *The Prelude*, XI, l. 305, in Wordsworth, *The Poetical Works of William Wordsworth*, p. 731.

26. Robert Langbaum, *The Poetry of Experience*, pp. 11–12.

27. See above, pp. 134 ff.

28. Langbaum, *The Poetry of Experience*, p. 11.

29. Charles Williams, "Wordsworth," *The English Poetic Mind*, pp. 153–71.

30. "Humility, Concentration, and Gusto," *Reader*, pp. 123–24.

31. *Ibid.*, p. 124.

32. See above, pp. 28, 35.

33. "Reticent Candor," *Reader*, p. 148.

34. W. H. Auden, "A Mosaic for Marianne Moore," *The New York Review of Books*, IX (Nov. 9, 1967), 3.

List of Works Consulted

Auden, Wystan Hugh, *About the House*, New York: Random House, 1965.

——— *The Collected Poetry of W. H. Auden*, New York: Random House, 1945.

——— *The Dyer's Hand and Other Essays*, New York: Random House, 1962.

——— "A Mosaic for Marianne Moore," *The New York Review of Books*, IX (Nov. 9, 1967), 3.

Barlow, T. D., *Woodcuts of Albrecht Dürer*, London: Penguin, 1948.

Beach, Joseph Warren, *The Making of the Auden Canon*, Minneapolis: University of Minnesota Press, 1957.

Beatty, Frederika, *William Wordsworth of Dove Cottage*, New York: Bookman Associates, 1964.

Blackmur, R. P., *Language as Gesture*, New York: Harcourt, Brace, 1952.

Bogan, Louise, *Selected Criticism: Prose, Poetry*, New York: Noonday Press, 1955.

Crane, Hart, *The Letters of Hart Crane*, ed. Brom Weber, Berkeley: University of California Press, 1965.

Current Biography, New York: Wilson, Dec. 1952.

Daiches, David, *Poetry and the Modern World*, Chicago: University of Chicago Press, 1940.

Eliot, Thomas Stearns, *Four Quartets*, New York: Harcourt, Brace, 1943.

Engel, Bernard F., *Marianne Moore*, New York: Twayne, 1964.

Fowlie, Wallace, "Marianne Moore," *Sewanee Review*, LX (July, 1952), 537–47.

Friar, Kimon, and John Malcolm Brinnin, eds., *Modern Poetry*, New York: Appleton-Century-Crofts, 1951.

Hall, Donald, "Interview with Marianne Moore," *McCall's*, XCIII (Dec., 1965), 74 ff.

Hardwick, Elizabeth, "Boston: the Lost Ideal," *Harper's*, CCXIX (Dec., 1959), 64–69.

Harrison, G. B., ed., *Major British Writers*, New York: Harcourt, Brace, 1959.

Hart, James D., *The Oxford Companion to American Literature*, New York: Oxford University Press, 1941.

Howard, Jane, "Leading Lady of U.S. Verse," *Life*, LXII (Jan. 13, 1967), 37–38 ff.

Jarrell, Randall, *Poetry and the Age*, New York: Knopf, 1953.

Johnson, Samuel, *The Lives of the Most Eminent English Poets*, ed. W. E. Henley, London: Methuen, 1896.

Keats, John, *The Selected Letters of John Keats*, ed. Lionel Trilling, New York: Doubleday Anchor, 1956.

Kenner, Hugh, "Meditation and Enactment," *Poetry: A Magazine of Verse*, CII (May, 1963), 109–15.

———— "Supreme in Her Abnormality," *Poetry: A Magazine of Verse*, LXXXIV (Sept., 1954), 356–63.

Kunitz, Stanley J., ed., *Twentieth Century Authors: First Supplement*, New York: Wilson, 1955.

Langbaum, Robert, *The Poetry of Experience*, New York: Norton, 1963.

"MacDowell Colony, 50 Years Old, Hails Marianne Moore," *The New York Times*, Aug. 21, 1967, p. 33M.

Milton, John, *Complete Prose Works of John Milton*, ed. Douglas Bush et al., New Haven, Conn.: Yale University Press, 1953– .

"Miss Moore in Manhattan," *The New Yorker*, XLI (Jan. 29, 1966), 24–26.

Moore, Marianne, "A Burning Desire to be Explicit," *Christian Science Monitor*, Jan. 11, 1966, p. 12.

———— *Collected Poems*, New York: Macmillan, 1951.

———— *The Complete Poems of Marianne Moore*, New York: Macmillan and Viking, 1967.

———— *Like a Bulwark*, New York: Viking, 1956.

———— *A Marianne Moore Reader*, New York: Viking, 1965.

———— *Nevertheless*, New York: Macmillan, 1944.

———— *O to Be a Dragon*, New York: Viking, 1959.

———— *Observations*, New York: Dial, 1924.

———— *Poems*, London: Egoist, 1921.

———— *Predilections*, New York: Viking, 1955.

———— "Religion and the Intellectuals," *Partisan Review*, XVII (Feb., 1950), 137–38.

———— *Selected Poems*, New York: Macmillan, 1935.

———— *Tell Me, Tell Me: Granite, Steel, and Other Topics*, New York: Viking, 1966.

———— *What Are Years?*, New York: Macmillan, 1941.

Nichols, Lewis, "Talk with Marianne Moore," *The New York Times Book Review*, May 16, 1954, p. 30.

Pearce, Roy Harvey, *The Continuity of American Poetry*, Princeton, N.J.: Princeton University Press, 1961.

Plimpton, George, "The World Series with Marianne Moore: Letter from an October Afternoon," *Harper's*, CCXXIX (Oct., 1964), 50–58.

Pound, Ezra, *The Letters of Ezra Pound*, ed. D. D. Paige, New York: Harcourt, Brace, 1950.

Rilke, Rainer Maria, *Duino Elegies*, tr. J .B. Leishman and Stephen Spender, London: Hogarth, 1957.

Sargeant, Winthrop, "Humility, Concentration, and Gusto," *The New Yorker*, XXXII (Feb. 16, 1957), 38–73.

Sassoon, Siegfried, *Collected Poems of Siegfried Sassoon*, New York: Viking, 1949.

Shaw, George Bernard, *Man and Superman*, London: Constable, 1931.

Sheehy, Eugene P., and K. A. Lohf (comps.), *The Achievement of Marianne Moore: A Bibliography, 1907–1957*, New York: New York Public Library, 1958.

Shelley, Percy Bysshe, *The Complete Works of Percy Bysshe Shelley*, ed. Roger Ingpen and Walter E. Peck, New York: Gordian, 1965.

Spiller, Robert E., *et al.*, eds., *Literary History of the United States*, 3rd ed. revised, New York: Macmillan, 1963.

Stevens, Wallace, *The Collected Poems of Wallace Stevens*, New York: Knopf, 1964.

——— *Letters of Wallace Stevens*, ed. Holly Stevens, New York: Knopf, 1966.

Tambimuttu, M. J., ed., *Festschrift for Marianne Moore's Seventy Seventh Birthday*, London: Frank Cass, 1966.

Tomlinson, Charles, "Abundance, Not Too Much: The Poetry of Marianne Moore," *Sewanee Review*, LXV (autumn, 1957), 677–87.

Trilling, Lionel, *The Liberal Imagination*, New York: Doubleday Anchor and Viking, 1954.

Weatherhead, A. Kingsley, *The Edge of the Image: Marianne Moore, William Carlos Williams, and Some Other Poets*, Seattle, Wash.: University of Washington Press, 1967.

Weber, Olga S., ed., *Literary and Library Prizes*, 5th ed., New York: R. R. Bowker, 1963.

Who's Who in America, Vol. 34 (1966–1967), Chicago: Marquis, 1966.

Williams, Charles, *The English Poetic Mind*, Oxford: Clarendon Press, 1932.

Williams, Oscar, ed., *New Poems 1940*, New York: Yardstick, 1941.

Williams, William Carlos, *Selected Essays of William Carlos Williams*, New York: Random House, 1954.

Wordsworth, William, *The Poetical Works of William Wordsworth*, ed. Thomas Hutchinson, London: Frowde, 1906.

Yeats, William Butler, *The Collected Poems of William Butler Yeats*, New York: Macmillan, 1951.

Index